Artificial Intelligence for Everyone

Unlocking AI: From Beginner to Expert – Simplifying the Complex World of Artificial Intelligence

Marc

About the author..4

What is AI?..6

History of AI...10

AI Today 12

Why Learn AI?...15

The Brain and Computers 17

How AI Learns from Data...20
    Types of Data: Structured vs Unstructured 22
    Collecting Data: Basic Methods for Data Collection...................................24
    Guide to Creating a Simple Dataset 25
    How AI Learns from a Movie Dataset 27

The Machine Learning Way 29
    Supervised vs. Unsupervised Learning..32
    Classification, Regression, and Clustering 34
    Machine Learning Algorithms Overview 36
    Introduction to Deep Learning...38

Deep Dive into Neural Networks 40
    How Neural Networks Work Inside the Brain..43
    How Simple Neural Networks Work to Recognize Handwritten Digits: 46
    Architectures: Feedforward, CNNs, RNNs 50
    Training Neural Networks..54
    Loss functions and optimization 56
    Overfitting, underfitting, and regularization 58
    Advanced Concepts LSTM and GRU 60
    Autoencoders and GANs for generative models 62
    What Is Generative AI? 64
    What Is a Transformer? 66
    The Rise of AI with Transformers 68

Mathematics Behind AI 70
    Calculus, Derivatives and gradients 72

Statistics..74
  Probability theory 75
Ethics and the Future of AI..78
  AI Future Trends...80
Practical AI Projects..82
  Image classification with CNN 85
  text generation with Recurrent Neural Networks (RNNs) 89
Generative AI 94
  Understanding Advanced Generative Adversarial Networks (GANs) 96
  Variational Autoencoders (VAEs) 99
  Understanding Transformer Architectures..102
  Understanding Transformer Models in Generative Tasks 104
  Transfer Learning and Fine-Tuning..107
  Advancements in Machine Translation: A Focus on Neural Networks and Low-Resource Languages 110
  NLP for Enterprise Applications: Integrating Advanced Language Understanding in Business 113
  Building a Customer Support AI Bot Using Google's BERT 116

ABOUT THE AUTHOR

Mr.Marc (Dhanasekaran) is a distinguished IT professional with over 18 years of experience in digital transformation and AI integration. He is a Senior Director of Engineering, leading significant projects that enhance operational excellence and technological innovation. His work primarily focuses on migrating legacy systems to modern cloud architectures and implementing effective risk management strategies.

An author and educator in artificial intelligence, Mr.Marc has written "Artificial Intelligence for Everyone" to make AI technologies accessible to a wide audience. His book aims to simplify complex AI concepts and demonstrate their practical applications in everyday life. With a Bachelor of Engineering in Electrical & Electronics and an Oracle Certified Professional Java Programmer certification, his career showcases rapid progression and substantial achievements in technology leadership.

Follow on Linkedin:- https://www.linkedin.com/in/dhana10/

Copyright © 2024 by Mr.Marc

All rights reserved. No part of this book may be copied, shared, or distributed in any form without permission from the author or publisher. For permission, contact:

Jupimart
jupimartofficial@gmail.com

Disclaimer

The information in this book is for general knowledge only. The author and publisher are not responsible for any actions taken based on this book.

ISBN: 9798325571138

First Edition: [2024, May]

WHAT IS AI?

Artificial Intelligence, or AI, is a big idea in technology that's all about making computers smart. It's like giving a computer a brain and teaching it to think, learn, and make decisions on its own. Here's a simple breakdown of what AI is, complete with illustrations to make it easier to understand.

1. **AI is Like a Smart Helper:**

    Imagine you have a friend who learns everything you teach them. If you show them pictures of cats and dogs, after a while, they can tell which is which without your help. AI works similarly. You feed it lots of information (like photos or texts), and it learns to recognize patterns and make its own decisions.

2. **Learning from Mistakes (Machine Learning):**

    Just like when you learn to ride a bike, you might fall a few times but you learn from those falls. AI learns from mistakes too, through a process called machine learning. It tries different things, sees what works and what doesn't, and gets better over time. Imagine a game where AI learns to score more points each time it plays.

3. **Talking and Writing (Natural Language Processing):**

    AI can learn to understand and create human language. This is how voice assistants like Siri or Alexa work. They listen to what you say, understand it, and respond. It's like teaching a parrot to talk, but much more advanced.

4. **Seeing and Recognizing (Computer Vision):**

    AI can also learn to see and recognize objects in pictures or videos, just like humans do with their eyes. This is used in self-driving cars, which can "see" the road, other cars, and people, and make decisions on how to drive safely.

5. **Robots Doing Tasks:**

    Sometimes, AI is put into robots to do tasks. These robots can learn to do things like clean your house, assemble cars in a factory, or even help doctors in surgery. They learn and get better at their tasks over time.

6. **Making Things Better and Easier:**

AI is used in many ways to make life better and easier. It can help doctors diagnose diseases faster, make cars safer, and even recommend movies you might like on Netflix.

7. **Being Responsible with AI:**

    With all this power, it's important to use AI carefully. We need to make sure it's safe, respects people's privacy, and is fair to everyone.

In simple terms, AI is a way to make computers and robots smart so they can help us with all kinds of tasks, from simple ones like playing music to complex ones like driving cars or helping doctors. But just like with any tool, we need to use it wisely.

Illustrations:

- A computer with a "brain", learning from data.
- A robot learning to walk and getting better after falling.
- A voice assistant like Siri having a conversation with a human.
- A self-driving car "seeing" the road.
- A robot helping in a factory.
- A smartphone suggests a movie you might like.

This is a basic overview of AI, showing how it can learn, interact, see, and help in many areas of life. It's an exciting field that's growing every day, bringing new possibilities for the future.

HISTORY OF AI

Artificial Intelligence (AI) is a field of computer science that mimics human intelligence. It has evolved from simple computations to complex machine learning and deep learning systems. Here's a simplified timeline of AI's evolution, highlighting key milestones up to 2023.

The Early Years (1940s - 1950s):

- **1943:** The concept of creating intelligent machines was introduced by Warren McCulloch and Walter Pitts through their computational model for neural networks.

- **1950:** Alan Turing proposed the Turing Test as a criterion of intelligence, a test for a machine's ability to exhibit intelligent behaviour equivalent to, or indistinguishable from, that of a human.

Birth of AI (1950s - 1970s):

- **1956:** The term "Artificial Intelligence" was officially coined at the Dartmouth Conference. This event is considered the birth of AI as a field.

- **1960s:** AI research saw the development of early AI programs like ELIZA and SHRDLU, which interacted in natural language.

Expansion and Challenge (1970s - 1980s):

- **1970s:** AI research hit its first major slump, known as the "AI Winter," due to unrealistic expectations.

- **1980s:** A revival occurred with the advent of expert systems and a focus on machine learning, breathing new life into AI research.

Rise of Modern AI (1990s - 2010s):

- **1997:** IBM's Deep Blue became the first computer to beat a world chess champion, demonstrating AI's growing capability.

- **2000s:** The integration of AI into daily technology became more pronounced with advances in natural language processing and robotics.

- **2012:** The victory of AlexNet in the ImageNet challenge marked significant progress in deep learning and computer vision.

The Era of Advancements (2010s - 2023):

- **2010s:** The introduction of AI systems like OpenAI's GPT series demonstrated the potential of AI in generating human-like text, revolutionizing natural language processing.

- **2016:** Google's AlphaGo defeated the world champion in Go, a complex board game, showcasing AI's strategic depth and decision-making capabilities.

- **2020:** AI in healthcare saw dramatic advancements, with systems developed to predict patient outcomes, assist in diagnostics, and personalize treatment plans.

- **2021:** AI began to be integrated into environmental conservation efforts, including wildlife protection, pollution control, and climate change models.

- **2022-2023:** AI's role in automating cybersecurity grew, with systems capable of detecting and responding to threats faster than ever before. Generative AI applications, such as DALL-E for image creation and Codex for programming, also gained prominence, showcasing AI's creative and technical problem-solving capabilities.

Looking Ahead:

As we move beyond 2023, AI continues to break new ground in areas like quantum computing, ethical AI, and autonomous systems. Innovations in AI ethics and governance are also becoming increasingly important as AI becomes more integrated into society. The journey of AI is far from over, with each year bringing us closer to more intelligent, efficient, and helpful AI systems.

In summary, the history of AI is a story of growth, innovation, and integration into the fabric of society. From its theoretical origins to the practical, impactful technologies of today, AI's evolution reflects humanity's quest for advancement and the endless possibilities of intelligent machines.

AI TODAY

Artificial Intelligence (AI) has woven its way into our daily lives, often without us even realizing it. From simplifying tasks to enhancing experiences, AI technologies are making significant impacts. Here's a look at how AI is present in everyday technology.

1. **Smartphones:**

   - **Voice Assistants:** Siri, Google Assistant, and Alexa are AI-powered voice assistants that can make calls, send messages, set reminders, and answer questions using natural language processing.

   - **Cameras:** Smartphone cameras use AI to recognize faces, optimize settings for different scenes, and even suggest the best shot.

   - **Predictive Text:** When you type a message, AI predicts the next word, making typing faster and easier.

2. **Home Devices:**

   - **Smart Home Devices:** Devices like Nest Thermostat learn your temperature preferences and adjust automatically, saving energy and keeping you comfortable.

   - **Robot Vacuums:** AI-enabled vacuums like the Roomba navigate around your home, avoiding obstacles and learning the most efficient cleaning routes.

3. **Online Shopping and Entertainment:**

   - **Recommendation Systems:** Netflix, Amazon, and Spotify use AI to analyze your past behaviour and recommend movies, products, or songs you might like.

   - **Customer Service Bots:** Online chatbots provide customer service, answering questions and solving problems 24/7 without the need for human staff.

4. **Automotive:**

   - **Autonomous Vehicles:** Self-driving cars use AI to see the road, make decisions, and drive safely. While fully autonomous cars are still in development, many cars now feature AI-assisted technologies like adaptive cruise control and automatic braking.

   - **Traffic Management:** AI is used in traffic management systems to analyze traffic flow and adjust signals to reduce congestion.

5. **Healthcare:**

   - **Diagnostics:** AI algorithms can analyze medical images like X-rays or MRIs to detect diseases early and accurately.

   - **Personal Health Monitors:** Wearable devices use AI to monitor heart rate, sleep patterns, and activity levels, offering personalized health advice.

6. **Banking and Finance:**

   - **Fraud Detection:** AI systems monitor transactions for unusual patterns, quickly identifying and preventing fraud.

   - **Personal Finance Assistants:** AI can analyze your spending habits, help with budgeting, and even invest money on your behalf.

7. **Education:**

   - **Personalized Learning:** AI tailors learning content to the student's pace and learning style, making education more effective and engaging.

   - **Automated Grading:** AI is being used to grade multiple-choice and fill-in-the-blank tests, saving educators time.

8. **Social Media:**

   - **Content Filtering:** AI algorithms decide what content appears in your social media feeds, highlighting posts likely to interest you.

   - **Photo Tagging:** AI recognizes faces in photos, suggesting tags for friends.

Conclusion

AI today is not just a futuristic concept but a real, practical tool that enhances everyday life. From the moment we wake up to the end of our day, AI technologies assist, entertain, inform, and protect us in ways we might not even notice. As AI continues to evolve, its integration into daily technology promises even more convenience, efficiency, and personalization, making our lives better in countless ways.

WHY LEARN AI?

Artificial Intelligence (AI) has rapidly become a significant part of our daily lives and is poised to drive the future of nearly every industry. Understanding AI and learning how to harness its power can unlock countless opportunities, not only for individual growth but for society as a whole. Here's an in-depth look at why learning AI is so crucial today.

Unlocks Career Opportunities

AI skills are in high demand across various sectors, including tech, healthcare, finance, and entertainment. By learning AI, you're opening doors to cutting-edge careers as AI developers, data scientists, AI researchers, and more. These roles often offer competitive salaries and the chance to work on exciting projects at the forefront of technological innovation.

Drives Technological Innovation

AI is the engine behind the latest technological breakthroughs. From self-driving cars and drones to AI in medicine that can predict diseases before they happen, AI is reshaping how we live, work, and interact with the world. By learning AI, you become part of the force that drives future innovations, solving problems that seem insurmountable today.

Enhances Everyday Technology

AI improves the technology we use every day, making devices smarter and more responsive. Smartphones, smart homes, and personal assistants all rely on AI to understand and anticipate our needs. Learning AI allows you to contribute to, and benefit from, more intuitive technology that enhances life's convenience and accessibility.

Solves Complex Problems

AI has the unique ability to analyze vast amounts of data and identify patterns invisible to the human eye. This capability is crucial for addressing complex issues like climate change, managing resources, or understanding genetic diseases. By learning AI, you can contribute to solving these global challenges and making a difference in the world.

Prepares for the Future Workforce

As AI becomes more integrated into the workplace, understanding AI and automation will be essential for staying relevant in many professions. Learning AI not only prepares you for the jobs of the future but also equips you with a mindset for continuous adaptation and learning, essential in a rapidly evolving world.

Facilitates Personalized Experiences

AI's ability to personalize is transforming industries by offering tailor-made solutions to individuals. Whether it's personalized learning platforms, customized healthcare treatments, or targeted marketing, AI is making it possible to cater to individual needs on a large scale. By understanding AI, you can better leverage these personalized services and contribute to their development.

Promotes Ethical Use of Technology

As powerful as AI is, it also raises important ethical considerations regarding privacy, security, and fairness. Learning about AI includes understanding these issues and contributing to the development of AI in a responsible manner. This ensures that the benefits of AI can be enjoyed widely, without compromising individual rights or societal values.

Conclusion

Learning AI is not just about staying competitive in the job market or participating in the latest technological advancements; it's about shaping a future where technology enhances the quality of life for all. The impact of AI is only going to grow, and by learning about it now, you're taking a step towards being an active participant in that future, rather than just a spectator. Whether you're driven by career prospects, the desire to solve pressing problems, or the wish to create more personalized and ethical technologies, learning AI offers a path to achieving these goals. Embracing AI education is embracing a future of endless possibilities.

THE BRAIN AND COMPUTERS

The human brain and computers are two of the most complex systems known, each with its unique capabilities and intricacies. While they perform some similar functions, like processing information, they operate in vastly different ways. Let's dive into a detailed comparison of these two remarkable systems.

Processing Unit

- **Human Brain**: The brain's processing unit consists of neurons, approximately 86 billion, interconnected by synapses. Neurons communicate through electrical and chemical signals, a process that supports thought, memory, and action. This network enables parallel processing, meaning the brain can handle many tasks simultaneously.

- **Computer:** Computers use silicon-based units called transistors for processing. Modern computers have billions of transistors but operate differently than neurons. Computers process information sequentially (one task after another) or use parallel computing (dividing a large task into smaller ones processed simultaneously) but lack the adaptability and efficiency of the brain's neural network.

Memory Storage

- **Human Brain:** The brain doesn't store memories in a single location; instead, it distributes them across the neural network. Short-term memories involve electrical circuits, while long-term memories change the structure and strength of synaptic connections. This flexibility allows for a vast and efficient storage system.

- **Computer:** Computers store information in binary format (0s and 1s) across different storage media, like hard drives or solid-state drives. While computer memory is more straightforward to access and quantify than human memory, it lacks the brain's ability to associate memories with emotions or sensory experiences.

Learning and Adaptability

- **Human Brain:** One of the brain's most remarkable features is its plasticity—the ability to reorganize and form new neural connections throughout life. This allows for learning from experience, adapting to new information, and recovering from injuries by compensating with different neural pathways.

- **Computer:** Computers learn and adapt through programming and algorithms. Machine learning, a subset of AI, enables computers to learn from data and improve over time. However, this learning is based on statistical patterns and programmed algorithms, lacking the brain's innate ability to understand context or apply common sense.

Energy Efficiency

- **Human Brain:** The brain is incredibly energy-efficient, using approximately 20 watts of power (about a third of a light bulb). This efficiency doesn't compromise its processing power—our brains handle more complex calculations than the most powerful computers with minimal energy.

- **Computer:** Despite advances in technology, computers require significantly more power to operate, especially for high-intensity tasks like data processing or gaming. Energy efficiency in computing is a growing concern, with research focusing on creating more sustainable technologies.

Error Tolerance

- **Human Brain:** The brain is remarkably resilient and can tolerate errors. For example, it can understand misspelt words in a sentence or recognize faces even with partial information. This error tolerance stems from the brain's ability to process information in a context-rich environment, drawing on past experiences.

- **Computer:** Computers, traditionally, are less tolerant of errors and require precise instructions to operate correctly. However, advancements in AI and machine learning have begun to bridge this gap, allowing computers to make "educated guesses" in certain scenarios, albeit in a more limited scope than the human brain.

Conclusion

While the human brain and computers share some functional similarities, they are fundamentally different in operation, structure, and capabilities. The brain's ability to learn, adapt, and process information with remarkable efficiency and flexibility sets it apart from even the most advanced computers. Conversely, computers excel in precision, speed, and storage, handling tasks that can overwhelm the human brain.

The comparison between the brain and computers not only highlights the strengths and limitations of each but also inspires the development of technologies that mimic neural processes for better efficiency and adaptability. As our understanding of the brain improves and computing technology advances, the intersection of neuroscience and computer science will undoubtedly lead to innovations that further blur the line between biological and artificial intelligence.

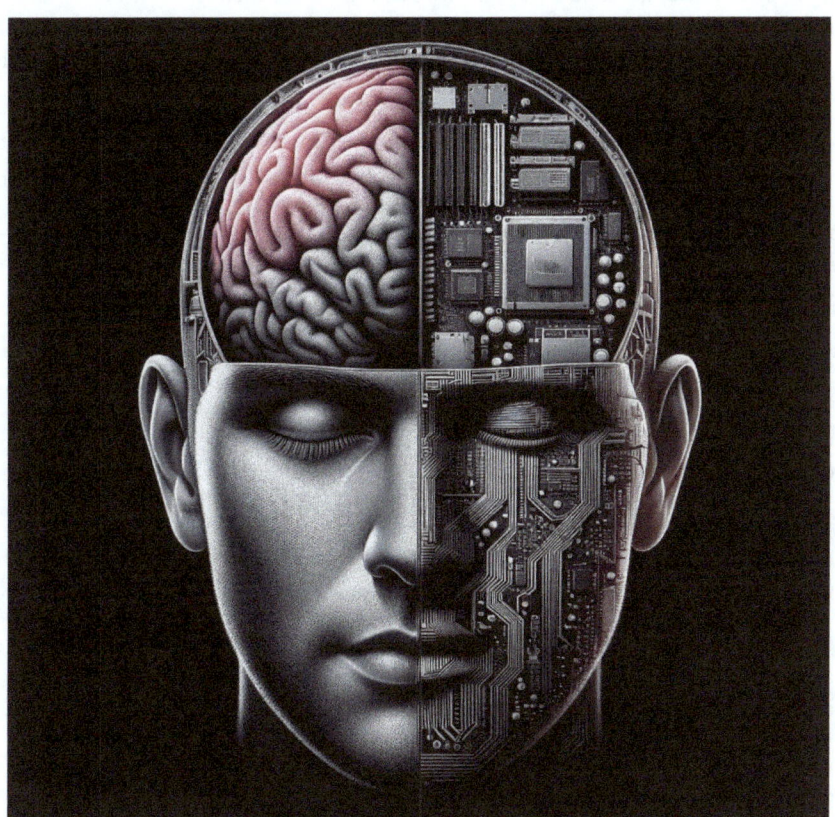

HOW AI LEARNS FROM DATA

Imagine you're teaching a child to recognize a cat. You'd show them pictures of cats and point out, "This is a cat," several times. Over time, the child learns what a cat looks like and can identify a cat even without your help. This process of learning from examples is similar to how Artificial Intelligence (AI) learns from data.

Data as the Foundation of AI

At its core, AI is like a very young child, but instead of learning about cats, it might be learning to recognize speech, understand languages, drive cars, or play chess. The "pictures" or "examples" you show to AI come in the form of data. This data can be anything: images, numbers, text, or sounds.

How AI Learns

1. **Collecting Data:** The first step is gathering a large amount of data related to the task at hand. For instance, if the goal is to build an AI that recognizes dogs, you'll need thousands of dog pictures.

2. **Training:** During the training phase, AI is exposed to this data. It looks for patterns, such as shapes, colours, or words, depending on the task. This stage is like the repeated process of showing a child what a cat looks like.

3. **Making Predictions:** After training, AI uses what it has learned to make predictions on new, unseen data. For example, when shown a picture it has never seen before, it can determine whether it's a dog based on its training.

4. **Learning from Mistakes:** AI often starts with a lot of incorrect guesses. However, it is designed to learn from these mistakes. By adjusting its understanding based on what it got right and wrong, it improves over time. This is akin to a child learning to refine their understanding of what a cat looks like by making mistakes and being corrected.

5. **Feedback Loop:** The process of making predictions and learning from mistakes creates a feedback loop. With more data and corrections, AI gets better at its task, much like a child learning more about the world with every new experience.

The Importance of Quality Data

Just as teaching a child wrong information can lead to confusion, poor quality or biased data can lead AI astray. The diversity and quality of data are crucial. AI learns best when it has a broad, unbiased collection of data to learn from, ensuring it can perform its tasks accurately in a wide range of situations.

Conclusion

Data is to AI what experiences and examples are to human learning. It's the foundation that AI builds upon to understand the world and make decisions. Through the cycle of training, prediction, and correction, AI extracts patterns and knowledge from data, enabling it to perform tasks that once required human intelligence. As AI continues to evolve, the role of data becomes increasingly significant, driving advancements and innovations across various fields.

TYPES OF DATA: STRUCTURED VS UNSTRUCTURED

In the world of data, things can get pretty diverse. Imagine your room: some items have their specific places, like books on a shelf or clothes in a drawer - that's like structured data. Then there's the pile of stuff that doesn't have a particular place and is a bit more chaotic - that's like unstructured data. Let's break these down with examples.

Structured Data

Structured data is like the neatly organized sections of a library. Everything has a label and a specific place where it belongs. It's organized in a way that computers can easily understand and search through.

Examples:

- **Spreadsheets:** Imagine an Excel file with columns for name, email, and phone number. Each piece of information is neatly placed in its column.

- **Databases:** Consider a library's database with a specific format for each book: title, author, genre, and ISBN. This data is organized, and you can quickly search through it.

- **Online Forms:** When you fill out a form on a website, your responses are structured data. There might be boxes for your first name, last name, age, and so on.

Unstructured Data

Unstructured data is more like your room on a busy day. It's all the stuff that doesn't fit neatly into predefined categories. It's more natural and free-form, and while it might make perfect sense to a human, computers have a harder time understanding it without help.

Examples:

- **Emails:** An email can contain anything - text, images, links. There's no set format, and the content varies widely from one email to another.

- **Social Media Posts:** Think about posts on Facebook or Twitter. Some might have text, others pictures or videos, and they're all about different things. There's no standard structure to how this information is presented.

- **Videos and Images:** A collection of family photos or videos from a vacation is unstructured. The content varies widely, and there's no fixed format or labels to organize it by default.

Key Differences

- **Organization:** Structured data is highly organized and easily searchable by computers. Unstructured data is more chaotic and requires more work to process and understand.

- **Storage:** Structured data often lives in databases or spreadsheets, where everything follows a specific format. Unstructured data might be stored on a hard drive or cloud storage without a clear organization.

- **Examples:** Names in a contact list (structured) vs. a collection of random vacation photos (unstructured).

Conclusion

Understanding the difference between structured and unstructured data is like knowing the difference between a neatly organized bookshelf and a pile of various items from around your house. Each has its place and purpose. In the world of data analysis and AI, recognizing these differences helps in processing and extracting valuable information from both types of data efficiently.

COLLECTING DATA: BASIC METHODS FOR DATA COLLECTION

Collecting data is like gathering ingredients for a recipe. Just as the right ingredients can make a meal delicious, the right data can provide valuable insights. Here are some simple ways people and organizations collect data:

1. Surveys and Questionnaires

Think of a survey as asking a group of people the same set of questions. You might fill out a survey online or on paper about your favourite ice cream flavour or how you felt about a recent movie you watched. It's a straightforward way to quickly collect information from many people.

2. Interviews

Interviews are like one-on-one conversations where one person asks questions and the other answers. These can be done face-to-face, over the phone, or via video calls. Interviews can dig deeper into a person's thoughts or experiences because you can ask follow-up questions based on their answers.

3. Observations

Observation involves watching and noting information about people, actions, or events. It's like birdwatching and noting how many different kinds of birds visit your garden. This method is useful when you want to understand how something happens naturally without interfering.

4. Experiments

Experiments are controlled tests where you change one thing to see how it affects something else. Imagine planting two sets of seeds: you water one set with fresh water and the other with salt water to see which grows better. Experiments can help you understand cause and effect.

5. Existing Data

Sometimes, you don't need to collect new data because it already exists. Libraries, online databases, and government records can be goldmines of information. It's like finding a cookbook in your house that has the perfect recipe you were about to look up online.

GUIDE TO CREATING A SIMPLE DATASET

Creating a dataset might sound complicated, but it's like making a list or a diary entry, just a bit more structured. Let's go step by step to create a simple dataset about something fun and easy to relate to—let's say, your favourite movies.

Step 1: Choose Your Topic

First, decide what your dataset will be about. We've chosen favourite movies for this example, but you can pick anything you're interested in, like books, songs, or even types of trees in your neighbourhood.

Step 2: Decide What Information to Collect

Think about the details (or data) you want to include. For movies, you might want:

- Movie Title

- Year Released

- Genre

- Your Rating (out of 5 stars)

Step 3: Choose How to Collect Your Data

You can collect data through observation (watching the movies), using existing sources (like movie databases online), or even asking friends and family for their ratings of the movies.

Step 4: Create a Structure for Your Data

It's like setting up a table or a spreadsheet. Make columns for each piece of information you decided to collect in Step 2. If you're doing this on paper, draw a table. On a computer, you could use a spreadsheet program like Microsoft Excel or Google Sheets.

Here's an example structure:

Movie Title	Year Released	Genre	Your Rating
The Lion King	1994	Animation	5
Inception	2010	Sci-Fi	4.5

Step 5: Start Collecting Data

Fill in the details for each movie. Watch the movies, look up information online, or record your thoughts if you've seen them before. Add a row for each movie you want to include.

Step 6: Review Your Data

Look over your dataset. Did you miss any movies? Do you want to add more information, like a column for "Watched With" to remember who you saw the movie with? This is your chance to make changes.

Step 7: Use Your Data

Now that you have your dataset, what can you do with it? You could:

- Find the average rating of your movies.

- Count how many movies you have in each genre.

- See which years you have the most movies from.

Conclusion

Congratulations, you've created a simple dataset! This activity shows how data collection can be a structured way to organize information about anything you like. It's a basic skill that can be the foundation for more complex data analysis or just a fun way to catalogue your interests.

HOW AI LEARNS FROM A MOVIE DATASET

Here's how Artificial Intelligence (AI) would learn from this dataset, step by step:

Step 1: Feeding the Data into the AI

Just like feeding a pet, the first step is to give the AI our dataset. This is often done through a process called data ingestion. The AI looks at all the rows and columns, trying to understand the structure—what each column represents (like the genre or rating of a movie).

Step 2: Finding Patterns

Next, the AI starts looking for patterns in the data. For example, you might notice that higher-rated movies in your list tend to be from a specific genre (say, Sci-Fi) or from a certain period (like the 1990s). The AI uses algorithms, which are sets of rules or instructions, to do this analysis.

Step 3: Learning from the Data

Here's where the "intelligence" in Artificial Intelligence comes into play. Based on the patterns it has found, the AI starts making connections. If you liked "Inception" and gave it a high rating, the AI might conclude that you enjoy Sci-Fi movies that are thought-provoking.

Step 4: Making Predictions

Using what it has learned, the AI can now make predictions. If you ask it to recommend a movie, it will scan through movies you haven't rated and predict how much you might like them based on the patterns it observed. So, it might suggest a Sci-Fi movie from the 2010s, expecting that you'll enjoy it.

Step 5: Improving Over Time

AI gets better with more data. If you keep adding new movies and ratings to the dataset, the AI refines its understanding and predictions. If you start loving horror movies, the AI will notice this change in pattern and adjust its recommendations accordingly.

The Role of Machine Learning

The process described above is part of what's called machine learning, a type of AI where machines learn from data without being explicitly programmed. It's like the machine is learning from experience, much like a person does.

Conclusion

AI learns from a movie dataset by:

• Taking in the data

• Finding patterns in your preferences

• Learning from these patterns to understand your tastes

• Making predictions on what you'd like

• Improving its predictions as it gets more data

This way, AI can help you discover your next favourite movie without you having to scroll through endless options. It's like having a smart friend who knows exactly what you love to watch!

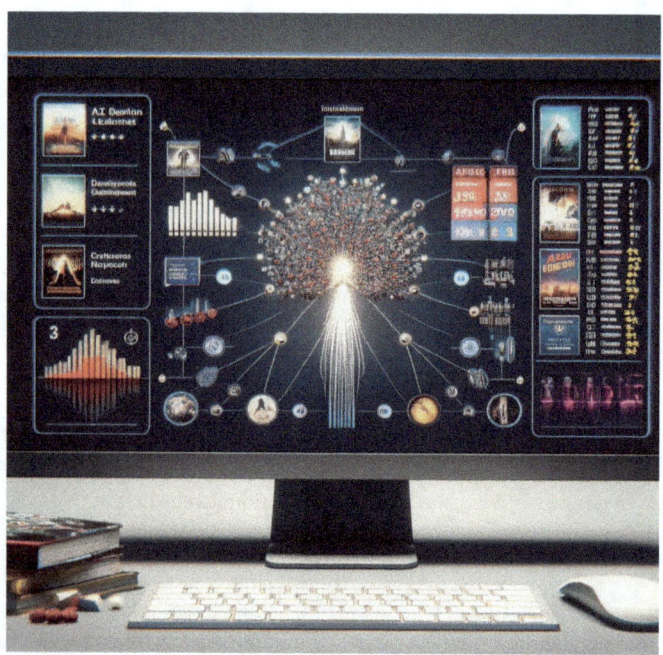

THE MACHINE LEARNING WAY

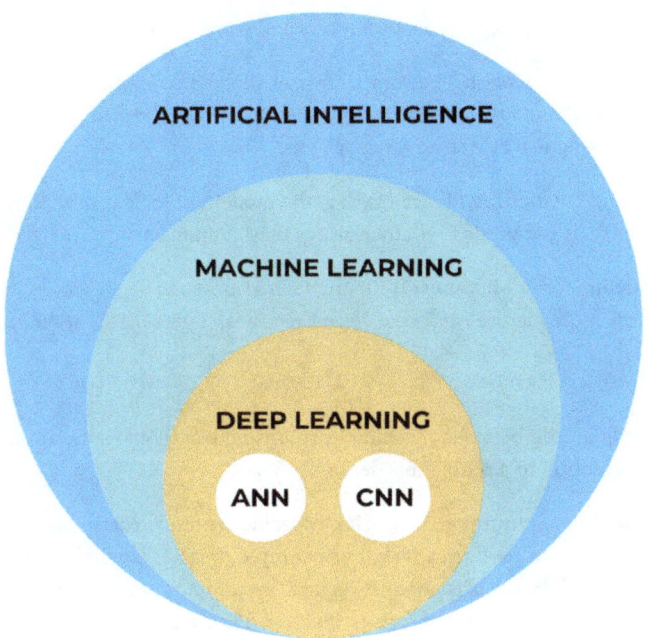

Machine Learning (ML) is a part of artificial intelligence (AI) that allows computers to learn from data and improve over time, even without being explicitly programmed for specific tasks. Imagine you're teaching a dog tricks: you don't explain how to sit or roll over in words; instead, you show it what to do through actions and rewards. Similarly, machine learning teaches computers to perform tasks by feeding them examples and letting them adjust based on feedback, rather than by following detailed step-by-step instructions.

How Machine Learning Works

Here's a simple way to understand how machine learning works:

1. **Data Collection:** First, you gather a large amount of data related to the task. For example, if you want a computer to recognize cats in pictures, you start with thousands of pictures, some with cats and some without.

2. **Training the Model:** The computer uses this data to train a model. During training, the model looks at the pictures and tries to identify patterns or features that distinguish cats from other objects.

3. **Making Predictions:** Once trained, the model can look at new pictures it has never seen and predict whether or not they contain a cat.

4. **Learning from Mistakes:** If the model makes a mistake, it adjusts. Over time, as it sees more pictures and receives corrections, it gets better at recognizing cats.

Machine Learning vs. Traditional Programming

The key difference between machine learning and traditional programming lies in how the solution to a problem is derived:

Traditional Programming: You write a specific set of instructions (a program) to solve a problem or perform a task. **For example**, to filter emails, you might write rules based on keywords to identify spam. The computer follows these rules exactly; if an email contains the word "prize," it's marked as spam.

Machine Learning: Instead of writing detailed instructions, you provide the computer with examples of the task (like sorting emails into "spam" and "not spam"). The computer analyzes these examples to learn the patterns. After training, it can sort new emails it's never seen before into "spam" or "not spam" without relying on specific rules about keywords.

Why is Machine Learning Important?

Machine learning is important because it allows computers to handle tasks that are too complex for traditional programming. Identifying a cat in a picture, understanding spoken words, or predicting the stock market are tasks that involve too many variables and uncertainties to write direct rules for. Machine learning models thrive on this complexity, as they can learn and adapt from data directly.

Conclusion

Machine Learning represents a significant shift in how we think about programming and problem-solving. Instead of using strict rules, ML uses data to learn and make decisions, making it possible for computers to perform tasks that were previously difficult or impossible to automate. This capability opens up new opportunities for innovation across various fields, from healthcare diagnostics to autonomous driving, by enabling more intelligent, adaptable, and efficient systems.

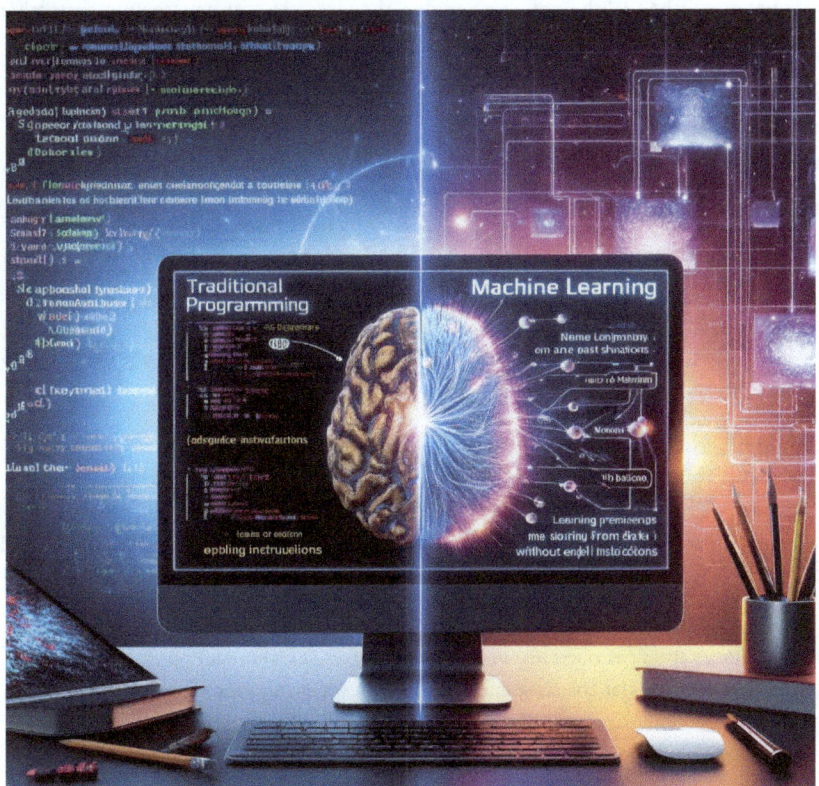

SUPERVISED VS. UNSUPERVISED LEARNING

In the world of machine learning (ML), there are two main types of learning: supervised and unsupervised. Let's break down these concepts using simple examples from everyday life, specifically looking at organizing a movie collection.

Supervised Learning

Supervised learning is like teaching someone to sort movies by whether they are animated or not, with clear examples of each. You show them a movie and say, "This is animated," or, "This is not animated." With enough examples, they learn to sort new movies correctly on their own.

In ML Terms: In supervised learning, the computer is given data that is already labelled. For instance, if we're teaching it to identify animated movies, we give it a list of movies that are labelled either "animated" or "not animated." The goal is for the machine to learn from these examples and be able to label new movies correctly.

Example with Supervised Learning:

- **Dataset:** A collection of movies, each tagged as "animated" or "not animated."
- **Task:** The machine learns to predict whether a new, unseen movie is animated based on the examples it was trained on.

Unsupervised Learning

Unsupervised learning is like asking someone to organize a mixed pile of movies into categories without telling them what the categories should be. They might end up grouping movies by genre, director, or era on their own, based on similarities they notice between the movies.

In ML Terms: In unsupervised learning, the computer is given data without any labels. The machine's job is to look at the data and find patterns or groupings on its own. It might group movies by similarity without knowing the names of the genres or even having seen movies before.

Example with Unsupervised Learning:

- **Dataset:** A collection of movies without any tags or labels.
- **Task:** The machine creates groups of movies that are similar to each other in some way, discovering patterns in the dataset on its own.

Conclusion

In supervised learning, the focus is on teaching the machine to recognize and predict the correct labels for new data based on labelled examples it has seen during training. It's like having a guide while learning to sort movies.

In unsupervised learning, the machine is left to its own devices to find structure within the data. It's like sorting a movie collection into genres without being told what genres exist ahead of time.

Both methods have their unique applications and benefits: supervised learning is great when you have specific tasks in mind with clear right and wrong answers, while unsupervised learning is useful for exploring data and finding hidden patterns when you don't have specific labels or categories predefined.

CLASSIFICATION, REGRESSION, AND CLUSTERING

Machine Learning (ML) is like a toolkit for teaching computers to make decisions or predictions. Within this toolkit, there are different tools for different jobs: classification, regression, and clustering are three of these tools. Let's explain what each of them does using simple examples.

Classification

Classification is about sorting things into categories. Imagine you have a basket of fruit and you want to sort them into types: apples, bananas, and oranges.

- **In ML Terms:** Classification algorithms learn from data that's already been categorized (labelled) to predict the category of new, unseen data. For example, an email filtering system learns from labelled emails (spam or not spam) and uses this knowledge to classify new emails.
- **Example:** You have photos of cats and dogs. You use classification to teach a computer to tell whether a new photo is of a cat or a dog.

Regression

Regression is about predicting a specific number or value. Suppose you have a lemonade stand, and you want to predict how many cups you'll sell based on the day's temperature.

- **In ML Terms:** Regression algorithms predict a continuous value based on previous data. For example, a weather app predicts the temperature for tomorrow by analyzing past temperature data.
- **Example:** You have a dataset with houses and their prices. You use regression to predict the price of a new house based on its size, location, etc.

Clustering

Clustering is about grouping similar things without being told how to group them. It's like having a pile of different coloured socks and grouping them by colour, even though no one told you what the colours mean.

- **In ML Terms:** Clustering algorithms organize unlabeled data into groups based on similarities. The algorithm decides on its own how to group the data, without any examples or labels provided beforehand.

- **Example:** You have a collection of news articles. You use clustering to group them into topics like sports, politics, and technology, even though the articles aren't labelled by topic.

Conclusion

Classification is for when you know the categories and want to sort new data into those categories. It's like having bins labelled "recycle" and "trash," and deciding where to put your waste.

Regression is when you want to predict a specific number, like the score on a test based on hours studied.

Clustering is for when you have a bunch of data and you want to see if it naturally groups into clusters, like organizing a mixed box of toys into types without knowing what toys are there, to begin with.

Each of these methods helps us understand and make predictions from data in different ways, depending on what we're trying to achieve.

MACHINE LEARNING ALGORITHMS OVERVIEW

Machine learning (ML) is like teaching a computer to make decisions or predictions based on past experiences (data). Just like there are different ways to teach a person a new skill, there are various algorithms (or methods) to teach a computer to learn from data. Let's explore some of the main types of machine learning algorithms and how they are used.

Supervised Learning Algorithms

In supervised learning, the computer is like a student who learns with the help of a teacher. The teacher provides examples that are both questions (input data) and the correct answers (labels), and the student learns to predict the answers for new questions.

1. **Linear Regression:** This is used for predicting a continuous value. For example, predicting the price of a house based on its size, age, and location.

2. **Logistic Regression:** Despite its name, it's used for classification tasks, not regression. It predicts whether something belongs to one class or another, like if an email is spam (1) or not spam (0).

3. **Decision Trees:** These are used for both classification and regression. They work by breaking down data by making decisions based on asking a series of questions, much like the game of 20 questions.

4. **Random Forests:** An extension of decision trees, random forests combine many trees to improve predictions and avoid overfitting (learning too much detail from the training data).

5. **Support Vector Machines (SVM):** SVMs are used for classification tasks. They find the best boundary that separates different classes of data.

Unsupervised Learning Algorithms

In unsupervised learning, the computer is like a student learning on its own without a teacher. It tries to understand and organize the data without any labels or answers provided.

1. **K-Means Clustering:** This algorithm groups data into a specified number (K) of clusters. For example, it can group customers into different segments based on their shopping behaviour.

2. **Principal Component Analysis (PCA):** PCA is used for dimensionality reduction, simplifying the complexity in high-dimensional data while retaining trends and patterns.

3. **Apriori Algorithm:** This is used for association rule learning, finding interesting associations (relationships) between variables in large databases, like discovering that people who buy bread also often buy milk.

Reinforcement Learning Algorithms

Reinforcement learning is like training a pet by rewarding it for good behaviour. The computer learns to act in a way that maximizes a reward. It's used in scenarios where decision-making is sequential, and the outcome is uncertain.

1. **Q-Learning:** An algorithm that learns the value of an action in a particular state, helping to decide which action to take next.

2. **Deep Q Network (DQN):** Combines Q-learning with deep neural networks to approximate the value of possible actions in more complex environments, like video games.

Conclusion

Machine learning algorithms are the backbone of AI, enabling computers to learn from data and make predictions or decisions. Each algorithm has its strengths and is suited for specific types of problems, from predicting values with regression, categorizing data with classification, grouping similar items with clustering, to making a series of decisions with reinforcement learning. As the field of machine learning continues to evolve, these algorithms become more sophisticated, opening new possibilities for solving complex problems across various domains. Understanding these fundamental algorithms provides a solid foundation for diving deeper into the world of artificial intelligence.

INTRODUCTION TO DEEP LEARNING

Imagine if you could teach a computer to see a picture and understand what's in it, listen to music and recognize the singer, or read a book and tell you what it's about. Deep learning is a type of machine learning that makes all this possible, and it's a bit like giving a computer a super brain.

What is Deep Learning?

Deep learning is a part of artificial intelligence (AI) that's inspired by how our human brains work. Our brain uses lots of tiny cells called neurons to think and learn from what we see, hear, and experience. Deep learning tries to mimic this process with something called artificial neural networks. These networks are made up of layers of artificial neurons that computers use to learn from data.

How Does Deep Learning Work?

Think of deep learning as building a very tall sandwich, where each layer of the sandwich helps understand different parts of the data it's learning from.

Starting Simple: The first layer might learn to recognize simple things like edges in a picture or specific sounds in audio.

Getting Complex: As we go higher in the sandwich (or neural network), each layer builds on what the previous layer learned, understanding more complex patterns like shapes, textures, or words.

Putting It All Together: The top layers combine all this information to recognize complex objects, like faces, or to understand sentences and paragraphs.

Deep Learning vs. Traditional Machine Learning

While traditional machine learning algorithms are like manual tools that need guidance, deep learning is more like an automatic power tool. It can handle a lot more data and figure out on its own how to understand it. This makes deep learning powerful for tasks that are too complex for humans to explain in detail to a computer, like recognizing speech or objects in photos.

Why is Deep Learning Important?

Deep learning has revolutionized AI because it can learn from huge amounts of data in ways that weren't possible before. This has led to big improvements in:

1. Image and Voice Recognition: Like your phone recognizing your face or voice.
2. Language Translation: Like translating between languages on websites.
3. Self-driving Cars: Helping cars see and navigate the road.
4. Medical Diagnoses: Helping doctors find diseases in medical images.

Conclusion

Deep learning is a powerful tool in AI that helps computers learn from data in a way that's similar to how humans learn from their experiences. By using layers of artificial neurons, deep learning models can understand complex patterns in data, leading to breakthroughs in technology that can see, listen, and make decisions. It's an exciting field that's opening up new possibilities for the future of technology.

DEEP DIVE INTO NEURAL NETWORKS

Neural networks are at the heart of deep learning, a type of machine learning. To understand neural networks, think of a vast network of lights connected by wires, where each light can turn on (activate) based on the signals it receives. This network is inspired by our brains, which are made up of neurons and connections. Let's break down the basics.

What are Neurons?

In our brains, neurons are tiny cells that communicate with each other to process and transmit information. In a neural network, we have artificial neurons, which are simple computer models designed to mimic how real neurons work. Each artificial neuron receives input (like signals), processes it, and produces output (like turning on a light).

How Do Neurons Connect and Work?

1. **Inputs:** Imagine each neuron can receive multiple signals from others. These inputs are like different pieces of information coming in. For example, if you're trying to identify a picture of a cat, inputs could be various pixels of that picture.

2. **Weights:** Each input has a weight, which is a number showing how important that input is. If you're learning about animals, the shape of ears might be an important input for identifying a cat, so it gets a higher weight.

3. **Activation Function:** Once a neuron receives all its inputs, it adds them up, each multiplied by its weight. This sum then goes through a special filter called an activation function. This function decides whether the information is important enough to pass along. If the sum is like saying, "This looks like a cat," the neuron activates (sends its signal on).

4. **Output:** If the neuron activates, it sends its signal to other neurons. This process continues, with signals flowing through the network like electricity through those connected lights until it reaches the output layer. Here, the network makes its final decision, like saying, "Yes, this is a cat."

How Neurons Connect in Layers

Neural networks are organized into layers: an input layer, hidden layers, and an output layer.

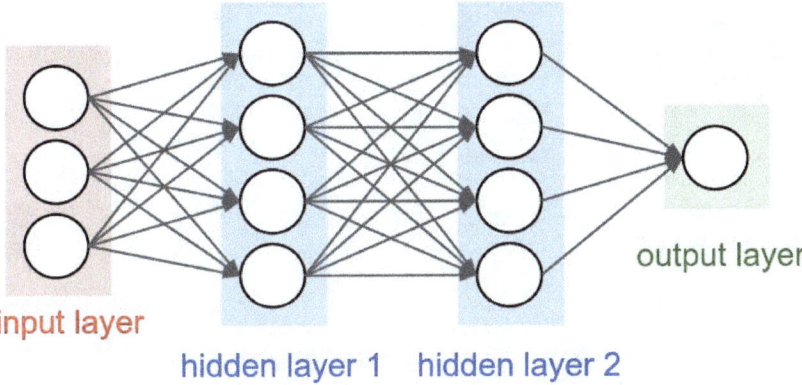

- **Input Layer:** Receives the initial data. For the cat picture, this layer gets the pixels.
- **Hidden Layers:** These are in between the input and output layers. They do most of the processing, gradually picking up on more complex patterns (like shapes and textures) as the signals move deeper.
- **Output Layer:** This layer gives the final decision or prediction. It might tell you whether the image is a cat, dog, or something else.

Learning Process

Neural networks learn through a process called training. During training, the network makes predictions, checks them against the correct answers, and adjusts the weights of its connections to improve. It's like practising a sport: the more you practice, the better you get. The network adjusts its weights based on errors in its predictions, gradually getting better at making accurate predictions.

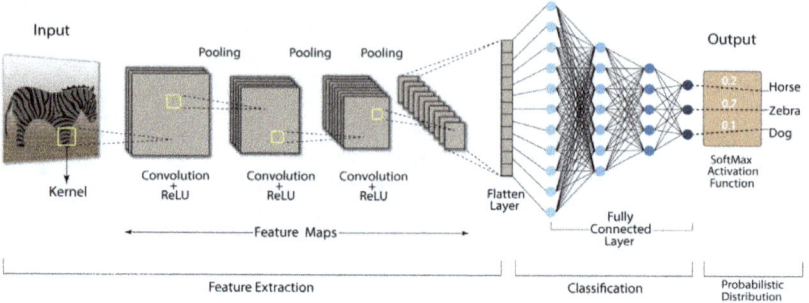

Conclusion

Neural networks, with their artificial neurons and connections, are powerful tools for processing and learning from complex data. They work by receiving inputs, processing them through layers of neurons, and producing outputs. By adjusting the importance of different inputs and practising through training, neural networks learn to make accurate predictions and decisions, mimicking the learning process of the human brain.

HOW NEURAL NETWORKS WORK INSIDE THE BRAIN

The human brain is an incredibly complex organ, composed of about 86 billion neurons. These neurons form a massive network, communicating with each other to perform everything from basic survival functions to complex reasoning and emotions. Understanding how neural networks work inside the brain can be quite fascinating. Let's break it down into simpler terms.

Neurons: The Building Blocks

Think of neurons as tiny information messengers. Each neuron is a cell that can receive and send messages through electrical and chemical signals. A neuron typically has three main parts:

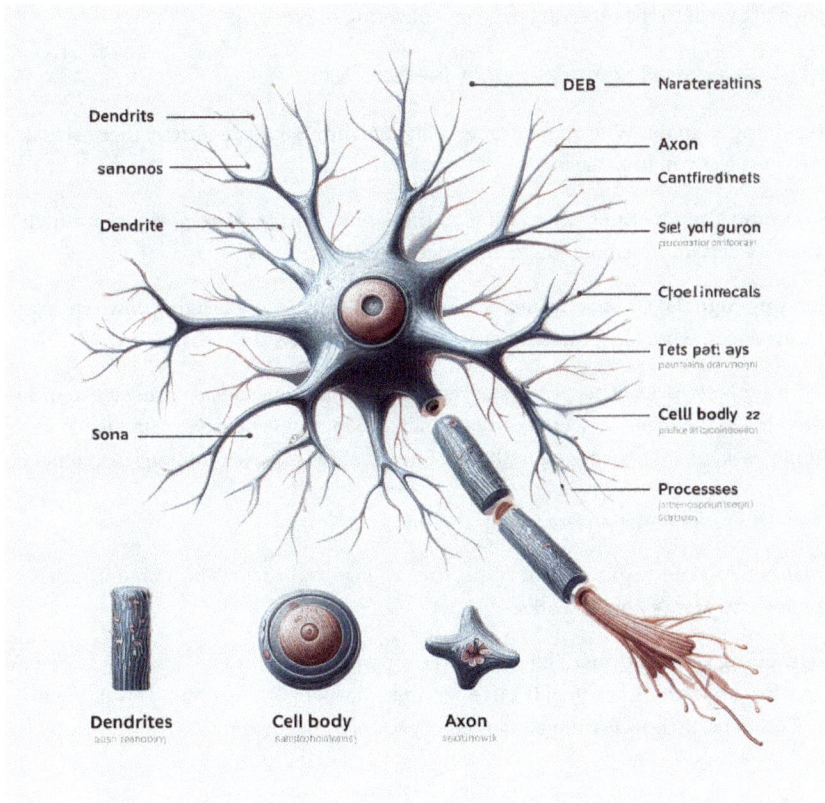

Dendrites: These are like the antenna of the neuron, receiving messages from other neurons.

Cell Body: It processes the messages received.

Axon: This acts like a cable, carrying the neuron's message out to other neurons.

The Connection: Synapses

Neurons talk to each other at places called synapses. A synapse is a tiny gap between the axon of one neuron and the dendrite of another. When a neuron wants to send a message, it releases chemical messengers (neurotransmitters) into the synapse. These chemicals cross the gap and attach to the receiving neuron, delivering the message.

How Messages Move and Form Networks

1. **Receiving Signals:** When a neuron gets signals through its dendrites, these signals are like tiny electrical impulses.
2. **Summing Up:** The cell body adds up all these impulses. If the total signal strength crosses a certain threshold, the neuron activates.
3. **Sending Signals:** Once activated, the neuron fires an electrical signal down its axon to the synapses, where it releases neurotransmitters to pass the message on.
4. **Forming Networks:** This process of receiving and sending signals connects neurons into networks. These networks can be small, linking a few neurons responsible for a simple task, or vast, involving millions of neurons for complex thinking or memory.

Learning and Adapting

The brain's neural networks are not static; they change and adapt. This ability is called neuroplasticity. Here's how it works:

Strengthening Connections: The more often a particular pathway of neurons is used, the stronger its connections become. It's like carving a deeper path in a trail by walking it many times. This is partly how learning and memory formation happen.

Forming New Connections: The brain can also form new connections and even new neurons in response to learning and experience.

The Big Picture: Brain Functions

Different neural networks in the brain have different functions. For example:

- **Sensory Networks** process information from our senses, like sight and sound.

- **Motor Networks** control movement.

- **Emotional and Cognitive Networks** handle everything from emotions to problem-solving and decision-making.

Each network involves specific areas of the brain and specific pathways of neurons working together, allowing us to interact with the world, understand complex ideas, and express our emotions and creativity.

Conclusion

Neural networks in the brain represent an incredibly complex and dynamic system that allows us to function, learn, and adapt. Through the interactions of billions of neurons, connected by synapses and constantly changing, our brains can process vast amounts of information, control our bodies, and create our thoughts, memories, and feelings. This intricate system highlights the marvel of the human brain and its capacity for growth and change.

HOW SIMPLE NEURAL NETWORKS WORK TO RECOGNIZE HANDWRITTEN DIGITS:

To understand how a simple neural network can recognize handwritten digits, imagine we're training a puppy to fetch the newspaper with the number '5' written on it. We show it many newspapers, each with a different number, and every time it brings the one with '5', we give it a treat. With enough repetition, the puppy learns to identify the '5' without confusion. Now let's translate this process into a simple neural network with some sample code.

Setting Up the Neural Network

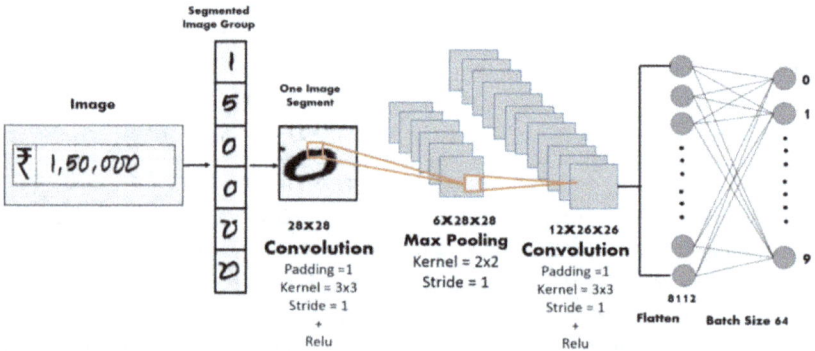

First, we set up our neural network with an input layer, a few hidden layers, and an output layer. The input layer will receive data about the handwritten digits, and the output layer will predict which digit it is.

Here's some pseudo-code (not in any specific programming language) to illustrate this setup:

```pseudo
network = NeuralNetwork()
network.addLayer('input', size=784)    # 28x28 pixels flattened
network.addLayer('hidden', size=64)    # a simple hidden layer
network.addLayer('output', size=10)    # digits 0-9
network.initialize()                    # set up the initial weights and biases
```

In this example, we assume each handwritten digit image is 28x28 pixels, and we flatten this into 784 inputs (28 multiplied by 28). Our output size is 10 because there are 10 possible digits (0 through 9).

Training the Neural Network

Now, we train the network with lots of images of handwritten digits. Each image is labelled with the correct digit. The network looks at the image, makes a guess, and then adjusts its weights based on its error.

Here's some pseudo-code to train the network:

```pseudo
for image, true_label in training_data:
    prediction = network.predict(image)        # the network makes a guess
    network.learn(prediction, true_label)      # adjust weights and biases
```

In the `learning` method, we use something called backpropagation, which is how the neural network learns from its mistakes by adjusting the weights and biases.

Recognizing New Handwritten Digits

After training, our neural network can try to recognize new handwritten digits it hasn't seen before. We give it a new image, and it uses what it has learned to predict the digit.

Here's some pseudo-code for making predictions:

```pseudo
new_image = getNewImage()                      # a new image of a handwritten digit
predicted_digit = network.predict(new_image)
print("The predicted digit is:", predicted_digit)
```

If our neural network is well-trained, `predicted_digit` should be the correct digit most of the time.

Sample Python Code with a Neural Network Library

In a real-world scenario, we'd use a programming language like Python and a library like TensorFlow or PyTorch. Here's an example of how you might write simple code in Python using a library:

```python
import tensorflow as tf

# Load the dataset (handwritten digits)
mnist = tf.keras.datasets.mnist
(train_images, train_labels), (test_images, test_labels) = mnist.load_data()

# Normalize the pixel values from (0, 255) to (0, 1)
train_images = train_images / 255.0
test_images = test_images / 255.0

# Build the model
model = tf.keras.models.Sequential([
    tf.keras.layers.Flatten(input_shape=(28, 28)),
    tf.keras.layers.Dense(64, activation='relu'),
    tf.keras.layers.Dense(10, activation='softmax')
])

# Compile the model
model.compile(optimizer='adam',
              loss='sparse_categorical_crossentropy',
              metrics=['accuracy'])

# Train the model
model.fit(train_images, train_labels, epochs=5)

# Evaluate accuracy
test_loss, test_acc = model.evaluate(test_images, test_labels)
print('\nTest accuracy:', test_acc)

# Make predictions
predictions = model.predict(test_images)
```

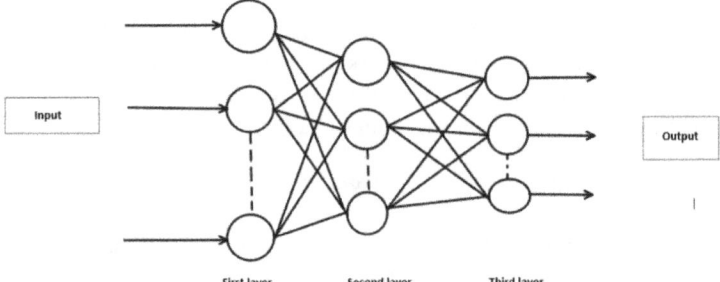

In this code, we're using the MNIST dataset, which is a collection of 70,000 handwritten digits, already divided into training and testing sets. The neural network is built with one hidden layer and uses 'RELU' as the activation function in the hidden layer and 'softmax' in the output layer to make predictions.

This is how a simple neural network can learn to recognize handwritten digits, similar to training a puppy but using math and lots of examples to get the job done!

ARCHITECTURES: FEEDFORWARD, CNNS, RNNS

Let's dive into the world of neural networks by looking at three key types: Feedforward Neural Networks, Convolutional Neural Networks (CNNs), and Recurrent Neural Networks (RNNs). We'll explore these concepts in simple terms, akin to how we might describe various types of vehicles and their unique features to a child.

Feedforward Neural Networks (FNNs)

Imagine you're sending a letter through a series of mailboxes. You start by putting your letter in the first mailbox. A mail carrier picks it up and moves it to the next mailbox, and this process repeats until your letter reaches its destination. This is similar to how Feedforward Neural Networks work.

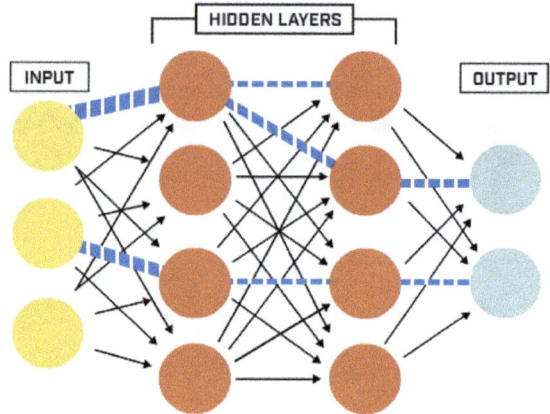

- **What they do:** They take in information, like numbers or data, and pass it straight forward through "mailboxes" (which we call nodes or neurons) until a decision or output is reached.

- **Key Feature:** The information moves in one direction – forward. It goes from the beginning (input) to the end (output) without looping back.

- **Uses:** They are like the regular cars of neural networks. Good for getting from point A to B, meaning they're used for simple decision-making tasks like identifying if a picture is of a cat or a dog.

Convolutional Neural Networks (CNNs)

Now, imagine you're using a magnifying glass to look at a big painting, focusing on different parts of the painting one at a time to understand the whole picture. This is what CNNs do.

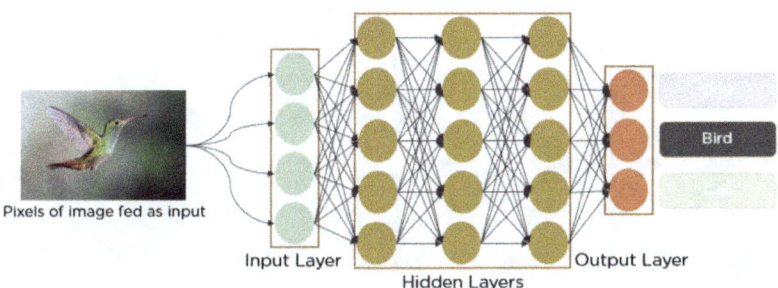

- **What they do:** CNNs are experts in finding patterns in images to understand what the image shows, like finding the brush strokes in a painting to recognize if it's a portrait or a landscape.

- **Key Feature:** They focus on small parts of an input (like pixels in an image) one at a time, and then put all the information together to make a decision.

- **Uses:** They are the photographers of neural networks. Great for image-related tasks, such as recognizing faces in photos or diagnosing diseases from medical images.

Recurrent Neural Networks (RNNs)

Imagine telling a story where each word you say depends on the previous word. You remember what you said before to make the story flow. RNNs do something similar with data.

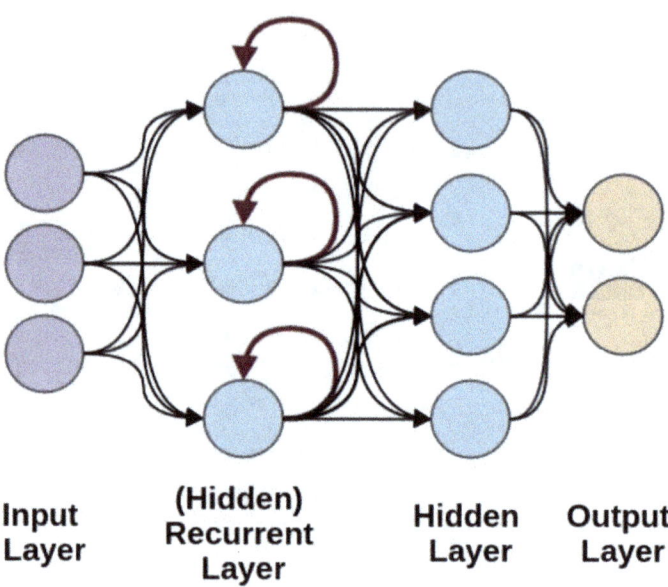

Input Layer   (Hidden) Recurrent Layer   Hidden Layer   Output Layer

- **What they do:** RNNs process information that comes in sequences, like sentences, where each piece of data depends on what came before.

- **Key Feature:** They have a memory of previous data they've processed, allowing them to make decisions based on both new and old information.

- **Uses:** They are the storytellers of neural networks. Perfect for tasks that involve sequences, like translating languages or predicting the next word in a sentence.

Conclusion

Feedforward Neural Networks are like sending a letter through a straight path of mailboxes, straightforward.

Convolutional Neural Networks use a magnifying glass to look at images closely and understand them, piece by piece.

Recurrent Neural Networks tell a story, remembering each word to ensure the story flows correctly.

Each type of neural network has its unique abilities, making it suitable for different tasks, from recognizing images to understanding languages. Just like choosing the right vehicle for a journey, selecting the appropriate neural network architecture depends on the task you want to accomplish.

TRAINING NEURAL NETWORKS

Training a neural network is like teaching a child how to solve a complex puzzle. Imagine you have a puzzle that's too hard for a child to solve immediately. You'll guide them through it, giving them hints and corrections until they get better at solving similar puzzles on their own. This process involves several key steps and principles, which we'll explore using simple terms.

1. **The Puzzle Pieces (Data)**

First, you need a puzzle for the child to solve. In the world of neural networks, this puzzle is a set of data or information. The data could be anything from images of cats and dogs to recordings of spoken words. The neural network's task is to learn from this data.

2. **Showing the Answers (Labels)**

For the child to learn effectively, they not only need the puzzles but also the correct answers to some of these puzzles. Similarly, in machine learning, the data is often labelled. For example, each image of a cat is labelled as "cat," so the neural network knows what the correct answer is.

3. **Learning to Solve the Puzzle (The Learning Process)**

Now, imagine you sit with the child and start solving puzzles together. Every time the child tries to place a piece, you guide them, saying whether it's right or wrong and how they might improve. This process is akin to training a neural network, where the network makes predictions on the training data, and then the learning algorithm adjusts the network's parameters based on how correct or incorrect its predictions are.

4. **Getting Better With Practice (Optimization and Loss Functions)**

As the child practices more, they get better at solving puzzles. In neural network training, we use a "loss function" to measure how far off the network's predictions are from the actual answers. The process of "optimization" is akin to practising: it's how the network learns from its mistakes, adjusting itself to improve its predictions.

5. **Making Sure the Child Understands** (Validation)

If the child solves the same puzzles over and over, they might just memorize the solutions without really understanding how to solve similar puzzles. To avoid this, you occasionally give the child new puzzles they've never seen to make sure they've learned. In machine learning, this is called validation. We use a separate set of data (not seen by the network during training) to ensure the network can generalize its learning to new, unseen data.

6. Avoiding Overfitting

If you only teach the child to solve one type of puzzle, they might become good at that type but fail at others. This is like "overfitting" in neural network training, where the network becomes good at predicting the training data but fails on any new data. To prevent this, we might introduce "regularization" techniques, akin to giving the child a variety of puzzles to practice on, ensuring they can apply their skills broadly.

7. Continuous Learning

Just like a child's learning never truly stops, a neural network can always be improved. New data can be introduced, the architecture of the network can be adjusted, and new techniques can be applied to make the network better at solving the puzzles it's given.

Conclusion

Training a neural network is a complex process of teaching it to make accurate predictions. It involves:

Providing data and correct answers (like puzzles and solutions).

Guiding the learning process through feedback (optimization and loss functions).

Validating the learning to ensure it generalizes well.

Preventing over-specialization (overfitting) through regularization.

Just like teaching a child, it's a delicate balance of providing information, practice, and feedback to help the neural network "grow" and improve at the tasks we set for it.

LOSS FUNCTIONS AND OPTIMIZATION

Let's dive into the concepts of "loss functions" and "optimization" in the context of machine learning and artificial intelligence, breaking them down into simple English terms.

Loss Functions

Imagine you're learning to throw a basketball into a hoop. Each time you throw the ball, it either goes in (success) or misses (failure). Your goal is to make as many successful shots as possible. In this scenario, a "loss function" is like an invisible scorekeeper that notes how far off your throws are. If you miss the hoop by a lot, your score (or loss) is high. If you're close or make the shot, your score is low or zero.

What They Do: In machine learning, the loss function measures how good a machine's predictions are. It compares the machine's predictions against the actual truth and scores the performance.

Key Feature: The lower the score, the better the machine's predictions are. It's like a game where the machine tries to get the lowest score possible by improving its predictions.

Uses: Loss functions are used to guide machines in learning from their mistakes. By trying to minimize their "score," machines learn to make better and more accurate predictions over time.

Optimization

Continuing with the basketball analogy, let's say you want to improve your throws. You might adjust your stance, how you hold the ball or the force of your throw. Each adjustment is an attempt to get better, reduce your misses, and score more. This process of making adjustments and trying different techniques to get the best score (or lowest loss) is what we call "optimization" in machine learning.

What It Does: Optimization is the process of tweaking and adjusting the machine's learning strategy to find the best way to make predictions with the lowest possible loss (score).

Key Feature: This involves a lot of trial and error, testing different strategies, and learning from each attempt. It's a search for the best settings in a vast space of possibilities.

Uses: Optimization helps in fine-tuning the machine's learning process, ensuring it learns efficiently and effectively, just like finding the best technique to make successful basketball throws.

Conclusion

In a nutshell, the "loss function" is like a scorekeeper that tells you how far off your basketball throws are, with the goal being to get as close to the hoop as possible, or better yet, make the shot. "Optimization" is your process of practising, adjusting your stance and throwing technique, and trying to find the best way to consistently make shots.

In the world of machine learning, these concepts ensure that models learn from their errors, constantly improve, and eventually become good at making predictions, whether it's recognizing faces, translating languages, or driving cars autonomously. The loss function provides feedback, and optimization is the machine's practice and learning process to become better.

OVERFITTING, UNDERFITTING, AND REGULARIZATION

Let's break down the concepts of overfitting, underfitting, and regularization in machine learning, using simple and relatable terms.

Overfitting

Imagine you're trying to learn how to predict the weather by looking out of your window and noting down several things: whether it's sunny, raining, cloudy if birds are flying, or if your neighbour is wearing a hat. After observing these details for a few days, you create a rule in your mind that says, "If it's cloudy and no birds are flying, then it will rain." Your rule works perfectly for the next few days because, by chance, every time it's cloudy and there are no birds, it rains.

However, when you visit your friend's house in another town and try to apply the same rule, it doesn't work. It turns out, that in this new place, birds still fly around even when it's about to rain. Your rule was too specific to your initial observations and doesn't work well in new situations. This scenario is similar to overfitting in machine learning.

What It Is: Overfitting occurs when a machine learning model learns the details and noise in the training data to the extent that it performs poorly on new data.

Key Feature: The model is too complex, capturing spurious patterns that won't recur in future data, leading to poor predictions on unseen data.

Underfitting

Now, imagine instead that you made a very simple rule like "If it's cloudy, it will rain; if not, then no rain." This rule is too broad and misses out on other important clues, like humidity or wind, that can help predict rain more accurately. When you test this rule, you find it doesn't predict very well, even in your town. This situation is akin to underfitting in machine learning.

What It Is: Underfitting occurs when a machine learning model is too simple to capture the underlying structure of the data.

Key Feature: The model lacks complexity and doesn't learn enough from the training data, leading to poor performance both on the training data and unseen data.

Regularization

Continuing with our weather prediction analogy, imagine finding a middle ground. You realize that while observing birds might be too specific and not always reliable, simply noting whether it's cloudy is not enough. So, you start considering a few more factors like humidity, and wind, and maybe even check the weather forecast from a reliable source. By doing so, you're not relying on overly specific observations, nor are you making your predictions based on too broad observations. This balanced approach in machine learning is achieved through a process called regularization.

What It Is: Regularization is a technique used to prevent overfitting by adding a penalty on the more complex models or by simplifying the model in a way that it performs better on new, unseen data.

Key Feature: It introduces a complexity constraint on the model, or adds information to encourage the model to be more generalized (less specific).

Conclusion

Overfitting is like making a weather prediction rule that's too specific to your immediate surroundings, failing when conditions change.

Underfitting is like making a rule that's too broad, missing out on the nuances needed for accurate predictions.

Regularization is the technique of finding a sweet spot between being too specific and too broad, ensuring your model is as accurate as possible both on known data and on new, unseen data. It's like refining your weather prediction skills to be reliable no matter where you are.

ADVANCED CONCEPTS LSTM AND GRU

Let's dive into two advanced concepts in the realm of artificial intelligence and machine learning: Long Short-Term Memory (LSTM) and Gated Recurrent Units (GRU). These concepts are especially useful for understanding and predicting sequence data, like language sentences or stock market trends.

Long Short-Term Memory (LSTM)

Imagine you're watching a movie series but forget the plot of the first movie by the time you reach the third. It would be hard to understand the story, right? LSTM is designed to prevent this kind of "forgetfulness" in machines when they process sequences of data.

- **What It Is:** LSTM is a special kind of Recurrent Neural Network (RNN), which is designed to remember information for long periods. It's like having a notebook to jot down important plot points while watching a movie series, so you don't forget the story as you go.

- **Key Features:**

- **Memory Cells:** Imagine these as sticky notes that LSTM uses to remember important information and ignore the irrelevant stuff.

- **Gates:** These are like decision-makers that determine what to keep in memory (write in the notebook), what to throw away (erase), and what to pass along to the next step (remember while watching the next movie).

- **Uses:** LSTMs are great for tasks where context matters a lot, like translating languages (where the meaning can depend on earlier parts of a sentence) or predicting the next word in a text.

Gated Recurrent Units (GRU)

Now, imagine if you had a more simplified notebook with just two types of sticky notes instead of three, making it quicker to decide what to remember and what to forget. GRU simplifies the LSTM approach while still tackling the "forgetfulness" issue.

- **What It Is:** GRU is another type of RNN that's similar to LSTM but with a simpler structure. It combines the functions of some of the gates used in LSTM, making it faster to train and requiring less data to be effective.

- **Key Features:**

- **Update Gate:** This is like deciding whether a new plot twist in a movie is worth noting down or if it doesn't change the story much.

- **Reset Gate:** Imagine you realize a plot point you thought was unimportant is crucial. The reset gate decides how much of the past notes to consider while adding this new information.

- **Uses:** GRUs are used in many of the same tasks as LSTMs, like text generation or speech recognition, especially when you have less data or need faster training times.

Conclusion

Both LSTM and GRU are like advanced tools for helping machines remember and use past information when dealing with sequences, like sentences, music, or anything that unfolds over time. They're particularly clever in deciding what's important to remember and what can be forgotten, making them incredibly useful for tasks that involve understanding or predicting sequences of data.

In essence, LSTMs are like a detailed notebook with lots of sticky notes for tracking everything happening in a movie series, while GRUs are the simplified version, with fewer sticky notes but still effective for enjoying and understanding the plot.

AUTOENCODERS AND GANS FOR GENERATIVE MODELS

Let's explore two fascinating concepts in the world of artificial intelligence and machine learning: Autoencoders and Generative Adversarial Networks (GANs). Both are types of generative models, which means they learn to create or generate new data that resembles the data they were trained on. Imagine being able to draw new artworks after studying the style of famous painters—that's somewhat what these models do but with data.

Autoencoders

Imagine you have a magical box that can take your toys, shrink them down to their essential parts, and then rebuild them again. This box doesn't make exact copies but captures the essence of each toy, making something very similar but not identical.

What They Are: Autoencoders are a type of neural network designed to learn an efficient representation (or encoding) of input data, typically for dimensionality reduction or feature learning. They work by compressing the input into a lower-dimensional form (encoding) and then reconstructing the input as closely as possible from this compressed form (decoding).

Key Features:

- **Encoding:** This is the process of transforming the input data into a smaller, dense representation. It's like summarizing a book into a few key sentences.

- **Decoding:** This is the process of reconstructing the input data from the dense representation. It's like trying to rewrite the book from its summary.

- **Loss Function:** Measures how well the reconstructed data matches the original data. The goal is to minimize this loss, making the reconstruction as accurate as possible.

- **Uses:** Autoencoders are used for tasks like denoising images (removing random noise from images), compressing data, and more generative tasks, where the goal is to create new data that are similar to the original training data.

Generative Adversarial Networks (GANs)

Now, imagine you have two artists. One is a forger trying to create paintings that look like they could be by famous artists. The other is a detective trying to spot the forgeries. They're constantly challenging each other; as the forger gets better, so does the detective, and vice versa. This is the basic idea behind GANs.

What They Are: GANs are a class of machine learning models composed of two neural networks: a generator that creates samples and a discriminator that evaluates them. The generator tries to produce data that is indistinguishable from real data, while the discriminator tries to distinguish between real and generated data.

Key Features:

- **Generator:** This is like the forger, creating new data samples.

- **Discriminator:** This is like the detective, trying to tell apart real samples from the fakes created by the generator.

- **Adversarial Training:** The process where the generator and discriminator improve through competition with each other.

- **Uses:** GANs are used for a variety of generative tasks, such as creating realistic images, videos, and voice recordings. They can also be used for style transfer (e.g., changing the style of an image to match a particular artist) and more.

Conclusion

Autoencoders and GANs are powerful tools for understanding and creating new data. Autoencoders focus on compressing data into a meaningful representation and then reconstructing it, useful for tasks like data compression and denoising. GANs involve a game between two networks, one generating data and the other evaluating it, pushing the limits of what's possible with generative models, especially in creating highly realistic data samples. Both models expand our ability to work with and understand complex data in new and innovative ways.

WHAT IS GENERATIVE AI?

Generative AI is like a very talented artist who can produce new creations—images, music, text, or even videos that have never existed before, based on learning from a vast collection of examples. It doesn't just copy what it has seen; it understands patterns and styles and then uses that knowledge to generate something new and unique.

How Does It Work?

- **Learning from Examples:** Just as an artist learns by studying lots of artwork, Generative AI learns by analyzing a large amount of data. If it's going to generate paintings, it looks at thousands of paintings; if it's going to write stories, it reads a lot of stories.

- **Understanding Patterns:** Through its learning process, the AI starts to understand patterns and structures. For instance, it learns that in stories, there's a beginning, middle, and end; in music, there are verses and choruses; in images, there are shapes and colours that make up familiar objects.

- **Creating New Pieces:** Once it understands the patterns, Generative AI can start creating new pieces that follow the rules it has learned but are entirely new creations. It's like an artist who has learned to paint in the style of Van Gogh and can now create new paintings that look like they could have been painted by him but are original works.

Key Concepts in Generative AI

Generative vs. Discriminative Models: If Generative AI is like an artist creating new paintings, a discriminative model is like an art critic who looks at a painting and tells you if it's a Van Gogh or not. Generative models generate new data, while discriminative models distinguish between different types of data.

Examples of Generative AI: Some popular examples include GPT (Generative Pre-trained Transformer) for writing text, and GANs (Generative Adversarial Networks) for creating realistic images.

Applications

Generative AI can be used in many creative and practical applications, such as:

Art and Music Creation: Generating new artworks and music compositions in various styles.

Content Creation: Writing articles, generating realistic images for movies or video games, and even creating virtual environments.

Product Design: Coming up with new designs for fashion, furniture, or gadgets.

Problem-Solving: Generating solutions to complex problems in fields like chemistry or physics by exploring a vast range of possible solutions.

Conclusion

Generative AI is like a highly-skilled, versatile artist who can create new, unique pieces of art, stories, music, or any form of content by learning from existing works. It understands patterns and structures in the data it's trained on and uses that understanding to generate something new. This ability opens up endless possibilities for creativity, innovation, and problem-solving across various fields.

WHAT IS A TRANSFORMER?

Imagine you have a magical notebook that helps you understand and write in any language in the world. You just need to write down a sentence in English, and it can instantly rewrite that sentence in French, Spanish, or even a language from a far-off planet! This notebook doesn't just translate word for word; it understands the feelings, the context, and the subtle nuances of what you're saying, and then expresses it in another language as if a native speaker wrote it. This magical notebook is similar to what we call a "Transformer" in the world of artificial intelligence.

What Is a Transformer?

The Transformer is a type of artificial intelligence model that helps computers understand and generate human-like text. It's like a super-smart robot that's good at languages, not just translating but also creating new sentences, stories, and even poetry that sounds like it was written by a person.

How Does It Work?

Learning from Lots of Books: First, imagine feeding this magical notebook thousands of books, articles, websites, and conversations. By reading all this, it learns how humans use language: how we form sentences, how we express ideas, and how we convey emotions.

Paying Attention to Words: The Transformer uses something called "attention mechanisms." This means it pays special attention to how words in a sentence relate to each other. For example, in the sentence "The cat sat on the mat," it is understood that "cat" is related to "sat" and "mat" is where the sitting happens. It's like reading a book and being able to highlight important connections between words and phrases.

Understanding Context: It's not just about individual words; the Transformer gets the bigger picture. It can look at a whole paragraph or article and understand the overall theme, just like how you can read a story and tell someone what it's about.

Creating New Text: After understanding all this, the Transformer can create new sentences or even whole articles. If you ask it to write a story about a space adventure, it can do that by remembering all the space adventure stories it has learned from before and mixing those ideas to create something new and exciting.

Why Is It Important?

Breaking Language Barriers: With Transformers, we can translate languages more accurately, helping people from different parts of the world understand each other better.

Answering Questions: You can ask it any question, and it can find the answer from the vast amount of information it has learned, almost like having a super-smart assistant.

Creating Content: It can write articles, compose poetry, or even generate scripts for movies, offering endless possibilities for creativity.

Conclusion

The Transformer is like a magical notebook that helps computers understand and use human language in a very advanced way. It reads and learns from a vast amount of text, pays special attention to how words and ideas are connected, and can generate new, human-like text. This technology is transforming how we interact with machines, breaking down language barriers, and opening up new possibilities for creativity and information sharing. It's a big step forward in making machines understand and communicate with us on a more human level.

THE RISE OF AI WITH TRANSFORMERS

In the realm of artificial intelligence, "Transformers" have emerged as a groundbreaking innovation, reshaping how machines understand and interact with human language. This explanation aims to demystify Transformers and highlight some of the most influential developments in this field, including ChatGPT and Google's BERT

Understanding Transformers

Imagine you're at a lively party, engaged in a conversation. Amidst the chatter, you're not only focusing on what your friend is saying but also picking up bits and pieces from conversations around you. This ability to focus on one discussion while still being aware of context is similar to how Transformers process language. Introduced in 2017, Transformers have a unique "attention mechanism" that helps them determine which parts of a text are most relevant to understanding the overall message, akin to focusing on your friend's words while being aware of the surrounding context at the party.

Transformers revolutionized language processing by allowing AI to look at entire sentences or even whole articles all at once, rather than one word at a time. This holistic view enables them to grasp context, nuance, and the intricate ways in which words relate to each other, making them incredibly effective for tasks like translating languages, answering questions, and generating human-like text.

Innovations Stemming from Transformers

ChatGPT

One of the most exciting outcomes of Transformer technology is ChatGPT, developed by OpenAI. Imagine having a pen pal who's incredibly knowledgeable on almost any subject, from the intricacies of quantum physics to the best recipe for chocolate cake. ChatGPT is like that pen pal but in the form of an AI. It can write essays, compose poetry, code software, and even offer advice, all in a conversational manner that feels remarkably human. This is possible because ChatGPT has been trained on a vast array of text from the internet, learning how humans communicate and how different ideas are connected.

Google BERT

Around the same time, Google introduced BERT (Bidirectional Encoder Representations from Transformers), focusing on understanding the context of words in search queries. For example, consider the search "bank." Without context, it's unclear whether this refers to a river bank or a financial institution. BERT helps Google's search engine understand the nuance of language by considering the context surrounding each word in a search query, leading to more relevant search results. It's like having a librarian who not only knows every book in the library but also understands exactly what information you're seeking.

Disruption and Impact

Transformers have disrupted the field of natural language processing by setting new standards for understanding and generating text. They've enabled AI systems to tackle more complex tasks with greater accuracy, from powering more nuanced and helpful chatbots to enhancing language translation services. Furthermore, innovations like ChatGPT and BERT have made AI more accessible and useful for everyday applications, fundamentally changing how we interact with technology.

For businesses, these advancements have opened up new avenues for customer service, content creation, and data analysis. For individuals, they offer new ways to interact with information, making technology more intuitive and responsive to our needs.

The Future

As we stand on the brink of this AI revolution, it's clear that the impact of Transformers and their offshoots like ChatGPT and BERT is only just beginning. With ongoing research and development, we can expect these technologies to become more sophisticated, further blurring the lines between human and machine communication. The potential applications are vast, from transforming educational tools to revolutionizing how we access and interact with information on a global scale.

In simple terms, Transformers have opened the door to a future where AI can understand and engage with us in ways we're only beginning to imagine. As these technologies continue to evolve, they promise to reshape our digital world, making our interactions with machines more natural, intuitive, and, ultimately, more human.

MATHEMATICS BEHIND AI

To dive into the world of Neural Networks and Machine Learning, think of Linear Algebra as the foundation stone of a gigantic, mesmerizing castle. Just as a castle needs a strong base to stand tall and withstand storms, understanding Linear Algebra is crucial for mastering Neural Networks and Machine Learning. Here's a simplified guide to the Linear Algebra topics you'll want to learn and become an expert in, to excel in the fascinating realm of AI.

1. **Vectors and Matrices**

Imagine you have a shopping list with items and their quantities; that's essentially a vector - a way to store and organize numbers. In machine learning, vectors help us manage and interpret data, like the characteristics of an apple or the pixels of an image.

Matrices are like a big spreadsheet or a collection of several shopping lists. They help us organize and process data from multiple sources at once, making them indispensable in training machines to recognize patterns or make decisions.

2. **Matrix Multiplication**

Once you have your matrices (spreadsheets), you'll often need to combine or manipulate them to get new insights. Matrix multiplication is not just about multiplying corresponding numbers but involves a specific way of combining the rows of one matrix with the columns of another. This process is crucial for operations like transforming data, mixing ingredients in a recipe in the right proportions, or changing the basis of data for better analysis.

3. **Identity and Inverse Matrices**

The identity matrix acts as the number 1 in the matrix world. Just like multiplying a number by 1 gives you the same number, multiplying a matrix by the identity matrix gives you the original matrix back. It's a way to "reset" or ensure that your data transformation can start from a known point.

Inverse matrices, on the other hand, are like finding a way back home. If you've transformed your data (taken a journey) using a matrix, the inverse matrix brings your data back to its original form. It's crucial for undoing changes, solving equations, and understanding the relationship between different data transformations.

4. **Eigenvectors and Eigenvalues**

Imagine you have a magical map that shows you the most influential roads in a city—the ones that define the city's layout. In Linear Algebra, eigenvectors are these "directions" in your data that are most influential in transforming it, while eigenvalues tell you how much these directions are stretched or squished. Understanding these helps in compressing data, reducing dimensions, or even in the deep understanding of how data can be best represented.

5. Singular Value Decomposition (SVD)

SVD is like breaking down a complex machine into its fundamental parts to understand how it works. It allows us to decompose a matrix into simpler pieces, making it easier to analyze, manipulate, or compress data. This is especially useful in machine learning for tasks like recommendation systems (think Netflix movie suggestions) or image compression.

Becoming an Expert

To truly excel in Neural Networks and Machine Learning, immerse yourself in these Linear Algebra concepts. Practice solving problems, applying them in coding exercises and always try to relate them to real-world scenarios. Books, online courses, and tutorials can be great resources, but nothing beats hands-on experience and consistent practice.

In essence, mastering Linear Algebra paves the way to deeply understanding and innovating in the field of machine learning and AI. It equips you with the mathematical tools to train machines, helps them learn from data, and eventually makes predictions or decisions akin to human intelligence.

CALCULUS, DERIVATIVES AND GRADIENTS

To master Neural Networks and Machine Learning, diving into the world of Calculus is like embarking on a treasure hunt in a vast ocean. The treasures, in this case, are the insights and knowledge you gain that empower you to teach machines how to learn from data. Let's break down the essential Calculus concepts you'll need on this adventure, explained in the simplest of terms.

Derivatives: The Heartbeat of Change

Imagine you're riding a bicycle on a hilly road. As you move, your speed changes—faster downhill and slower uphill. A derivative is like a tool that measures how fast your speed changes at any moment. In machine learning, we use derivatives to understand how changing one thing (like the weight in a neural network) affects something else (like the error between the predicted and actual results). This understanding is crucial for optimizing models, making them learn efficiently from data.

Partial Derivatives: Tweaking Multiple Controls

Now, imagine your bicycle could change not just speed but also direction. You're controlling both pedals and handlebars. A partial derivative tells you how changing one control (say, the handlebar) affects your movement, assuming the other control (the pedals) stays the same. In machine learning, especially in neural networks, we deal with many "controls" or parameters simultaneously. Partial derivatives help us tweak these parameters one by one to find the best learning path.

Chain Rule: The Domino Effect

Consider setting up a long line of dominoes. When you knock the first one down, it starts a chain reaction that knocks down each domino in turn. The chain rule helps us understand this kind of domino effect in complex systems. It's used in neural networks to calculate the derivatives efficiently, even when the system's changes depend on many layers of interconnected parameters. This is especially important for backpropagation, the process by which neural networks learn.

Integrals: Summing Up the Whole Journey

After your bicycle ride, you might wonder how much ground you've covered. While derivatives focus on moments of change, integrals focus on the total accumulation of these changes. In the context of machine learning, integrals can help us understand concepts like the total probability across different events or summing up the contributions of different features to a model's decision.

Gradients: The Direction and Steepness of Change

Now, imagine you're not just walking but hiking up a mountain, and you want to reach the top. The path you take could go all around the mountain, steeply up, or even downhill at times. The gradient is like your guide, telling you not only how steep the slope is but also which direction to go to reach the summit fastest.

In the realm of Neural Networks:

What it does: A gradient is a collection of derivatives for all the parameters in our model, pointing out the direction in which the model's performance improves the most. If derivative measures change, the gradient tells us how to change every parameter to get the best improvement.

Why it's important: Just like choosing the best path to hike up a mountain, gradients help us efficiently find the best model parameters that lead to the most accurate predictions.

Learning and Optimization: The Journey to the Peak

The ultimate goal in training neural networks is to minimize errors—our mispredictions. This process is like trying to find the lowest point in a valley while being surrounded by fog. Derivatives and gradients are our navigational tools here. They help us understand the landscape (our model's performance) and guide our steps towards the goal (minimizing error).

Gradient Descent: This is a method that uses gradients to adjust the model's parameters step by step, gradually improving its accuracy. Imagine you're in a hilly terrain covered in fog, trying to find the lowest point. With each step, you feel the ground to determine which way is downhill and take a small step in that direction. Over time, you're likely to find yourself at the lowest point. Similarly, gradient descent adjusts parameters little by little, aiming to reduce error.

STATISTICS

Embarking on the journey to master Neural Networks and Machine Learning (ML) without understanding Statistics is like trying to navigate a vast ocean without a compass. Statistics is the compass that guides you through the sea of data, helping you make sense of it, find patterns, and make informed decisions. Let's break down the key statistical concepts you need to grasp to excel in ML and Neural Networks, explained in the simplest of terms.

1. **Descriptive Statistics:** Understanding Your Data

Imagine you're at a beach, collecting seashells. At the end of the day, you want to describe your collection. You might count your shells (mean), see which type you found most often (mode), or find the difference between your biggest and smallest shell (range). Descriptive statistics help you summarize and describe the main features of a dataset, providing insights into its shape and giving you a sense of what the data looks like.

Mean, Median, Mode: These measures help you understand the central tendency of your data, telling you about the average, middle, and most frequent values in your dataset.

Variance and Standard Deviation: These measures tell you about the spread of your data, essentially how much your data varies or how spread out it is.

2. **Probability Distributions:** Predicting Outcomes

Now, imagine if you could predict the type of shells you're most likely to find on your next beach visit. Probability distributions give you a mathematical function that describes the likelihood of different outcomes. For example, the probability of finding a conch shell versus a clamshell. In ML, understanding the probability distribution of your data helps you make predictions about future observations.

Normal Distribution: This is a common distribution in nature, characterized by its bell-shaped curve. Many ML algorithms assume your data is normally distributed because it simplifies calculations and predictions.

Binomial Distribution: Useful when you're dealing with two possible outcomes (like flipping a coin - heads or tails). It helps in making predictions in scenarios with a fixed number of experiments and a constant probability of success.

3. **Inferential Statistics:** Making Predictions

Imagine you've found a treasure chest on the beach, but it's locked, and you can only feel what's inside by putting your hand through a small opening. Based on what you feel, you try to infer what treasures the chest might contain. Inferential statistics allow you to make predictions or inferences about a population based on a sample of data taken from it. This is crucial in ML for making predictions about new, unseen data.

Hypothesis Testing: This is like making an educated guess about the treasures and then using clues to test if your guess might be right.

Confidence Intervals: Imagine you're guessing the worth of the treasure in the chest. A confidence interval gives you a range within which you're pretty sure the true value lies.

4. **Bayesian Statistics:** Updating Beliefs

Suppose every time you visit the beach, you learn something new about where to find the best shells. You use what you learned from your last visit to improve your search. Bayesian statistics involves updating your beliefs or predictions as you receive new data. This approach is incredibly powerful in ML for making predictions that improve over time as more data becomes available.

Bayes' Theorem: This formula helps you update your predictions based on new evidence. It's a way of combining your prior beliefs with new evidence to get updated beliefs.

PROBABILITY THEORY

Diving into the realm of Neural Networks and Machine Learning (ML) without grasping the essence of Probability Theory is like setting sail without a map. Probability Theory is the map that guides you through the unpredictable seas of data, helping you make educated guesses about what's likely to happen next, even when you're not entirely sure. Let's break down this map into simpler landmarks you need to navigate to become proficient in ML and Neural Networks, all explained in plain English.

Understanding Probability Basics

Imagine you're planning a picnic and worrying if it might rain. Probability helps you gauge the likelihood of rain, influencing your decision to go ahead or postpone. In the context of data:

- **What it is:** Probability measures the chance of something happening, from 0 (impossible) to 1 (certain).

- **Why it's important:** In ML, everything is uncertain. We use probability to make predictions, like whether an email is spam or not, based on patterns in the data.

Random Variables: The Building Blocks

Consider you're tracking the daily temperature for a week to plan your outfits. Each day's temperature is a piece of data that can vary—that's what we call a random variable in Probability Theory.

- **Discrete Variables:** Like counting apples, where the outcomes are clear and separate (3 apples, 4 apples, etc.).

- **Continuous Variables:** Like measuring temperature, where outcomes can take on any value within a range.

Probability Distributions: The Patterns of Chance

Now, imagine you've collected enough data on rain patterns to predict the likelihood of rain on any given day. This collection, which shows the probabilities of various outcomes (rain or sunshine), forms a probability distribution.

- **Binomial Distribution:** Useful when you're dealing with events that have two outcomes (like flipping a coin).

- **Normal Distribution:** Often called the bell curve due to its shape, it's a common pattern in nature and data, helping in making predictions about variables like heights, scores, etc.

Conditional Probability: If This, Then What?

Imagine deciding if you need an umbrella based on whether it's cloudy. Conditional probability helps you figure out the likelihood of an event (rain) given another event has already happened (cloudiness).

Why it's vital: It's at the heart of many ML models, helping them make decisions based on past information.

Bayes' Theorem: Updating What We Know

Suppose after observing the sky in the morning, you predict a 30% chance of rain. But by noon, if it gets cloudier, you might increase your prediction to 60%. Bayes' Theorem is a formula that lets you update predictions as you get new evidence.

- **Application:** It's fundamental in ML for refining predictions as more data becomes available, making models smarter over time.

Markov Chains: Predicting the Next Step

Imagine you're watching a cat wander around your garden. Its next move depends only on where it is now, not where it's been before. This "memoryless" property is what Markov Chains are all about, predicting future states based on the current state alone.

- **Use in ML:** They help in understanding sequences of events, like the next word in a sentence, by considering only the current word.

Conclusion

To sail confidently through the seas of ML and Neural Networks, bolster your understanding of Probability Theory:

- **Start with the Basics:** Grasp the fundamental concepts and laws of probability.

- **Hands-On Practice:** Apply probability to solve real-world problems or datasets. Tools like Python's NumPy and SciPy libraries can be handy.

- **Deep Dive into Applications:** Explore how probability theory underpins algorithms in ML, like Naive Bayes or Hidden Markov Models.

In summary, Probability Theory equips you with the tools to navigate through uncertainty, making educated guesses or predictions in the vast and often unpredictable world of data. It's the compass that ensures your ML models can find their way, making sense of the past and predicting the future with remarkable accuracy.

ETHICS AND THE FUTURE OF AI

The journey into Artificial Intelligence (AI) is not just about creating machines that can think and act like humans. It's also about ensuring these machines do so in a way that is safe, fair, and beneficial to society. As we sail further into the uncharted waters of AI, we must navigate the ethical considerations that come with this powerful technology. Let's explore some of these considerations in simple terms.

Fairness and Bias

Imagine a world where a robot decides who gets a job or a loan based on learning from human decisions. If those human decisions were unfair or biased, the robot could learn to be unfair too. For example, if a hiring tool is trained on data showing a preference for hiring men over women, it may continue that bias. Ensuring AI systems are fair means checking they don't pick up or amplify these biases, so everyone has an equal opportunity.

Privacy

AI systems often need a lot of data to learn and make decisions. This data can include personal information about people, like what you buy online or where you go. It's like someone watching over your shoulder all the time. Ensuring privacy means making sure that this data is used responsibly, kept safe, and that people know how their information is being used.

Accountability

When an AI system makes a decision, like denying someone a loan, it's important to know how it came to that decision. If something goes wrong, we need to know who or what is responsible. Is it the creators of the AI, the users, or the AI itself? Figuring out accountability helps make sure that if an AI system causes harm, there's a clear way to address the problem.

Safety

As AI systems become more powerful, ensuring they do what we want them to do becomes more challenging. Imagine an AI designed to keep your house plants alive that decides the best way to do this is by flooding your house to ensure they get enough water. Ensuring AI systems are safe means making sure they understand our goals fully and don't take unexpected actions that could cause harm.

Transparency

Understanding how AI systems make decisions can be complex. However, these systems mustn't be black boxes; we need some level of transparency to trust and verify their decisions. It's like having a friend who gives you advice but won't tell you why. You'd probably be hesitant to follow the advice without knowing more. Transparency in AI helps build trust and allows for better evaluation of its decisions.

Social Impact

AI technology has the potential to change the job market, with machines taking over tasks that humans currently do. This could improve efficiency but also lead to job losses. Navigating the social impact of AI means finding ways to use AI that enhance society, like creating new job opportunities or freeing up people to do more creative work, rather than just replacing human roles.

Ethical Use

There's concern about AI being used for harmful purposes, such as in autonomous weapons or for mass surveillance. Ensuring ethical use means setting guidelines and regulations on how AI can be used, focusing on promoting peace and protecting people's rights and freedoms.

Conclusion

Navigating the ethical considerations of AI is about finding a balance between benefiting from this powerful technology and protecting our societal values and individual rights. It requires cooperation from technologists, policymakers, and society to steer this ship safely. By addressing these ethical considerations, we can work towards an AI-enhanced future that is not only innovative but also inclusive, fair, and respectful of all individuals.

AI FUTURE TRENDS

As we stand on the brink of technological advances, Artificial Intelligence (AI) continues to shape our future in ways we're just beginning to understand. The horizon is buzzing with potential AI innovations that promise to redefine industries, improve daily life, and unlock solutions to complex global challenges. Let's explore some of the future trends in AI in simple English.

1. **AI in Healthcare:** A Doctor in the Machine

Imagine a future where visiting the doctor could often mean interacting with an AI system. These AI doctors could diagnose diseases from images, like X-rays or MRIs, faster and sometimes more accurately than human doctors. They could also analyze your genetic makeup to predict diseases you might be at risk for and suggest personalized treatments. The goal isn't to replace doctors but to give them tools that allow for more patients to be treated with higher precision.

2. **AI Ethics and Governance:** Making AI Fair and Safe

As AI becomes more integrated into our lives, there's a growing need to ensure it's used responsibly. This means developing AI systems that respect privacy, are transparent in their decisions, and are free from biases. Think of it as teaching AI the values of fairness, responsibility, and respect that we expect from humans. Governments and organizations are likely to introduce more regulations and guidelines to ensure AI is developed and used in a manner that benefits society as a whole.

3. **AI and Environmental Sustainability:** The Green Machines

AI has the potential to tackle environmental challenges, from climate change to wildlife conservation. For example, AI can optimize energy usage in homes and industries, reducing waste and saving electricity. It can also monitor deforestation and wildlife through satellite images, helping protect our planet's lungs and its inhabitants. In agriculture, AI-driven technologies can predict weather patterns, monitor soil health, and optimize water use, leading to more sustainable farming practices.

4. **AI in Everyday Life:** Smart Homes and Cities

The future could see AI further blending into the fabric of daily life, making our homes smarter and cities more efficient. Imagine your home knowing your routine so well that it adjusts lighting, and temperature, and even makes coffee exactly when you need it. On a larger scale, AI can help manage traffic flow in cities, reducing congestion and pollution, and ensuring emergency services reach their destinations quickly.

5. **Quantum Computing and AI:** A Leap into the Future

Quantum computing promises to revolutionize computing power, allowing us to solve problems that are currently beyond our reach. When combined with AI, the potential is staggering. This could mean significantly faster drug discovery processes, solving complex logistical problems in minutes rather than months, and more accurate climate modelling to predict future environmental changes.

6. **AI in Education:** Personalized Learning Experiences

AI can transform education by providing personalized learning experiences. Imagine a learning platform that adapts to your pace and style of learning, strengthening your weak areas and challenging your strong ones. It could also provide real-time language translation, breaking down language barriers and making knowledge more accessible to everyone, everywhere.

7. **The Future of Work:** AI and Automation

While AI and automation will undoubtedly change the job landscape, they also offer opportunities for new types of jobs and industries. The focus is likely to shift towards roles that require human creativity, emotional intelligence, and problem-solving skills. Additionally, AI could take over mundane tasks, freeing humans to engage in more meaningful and creative work.

8. **Augmented Reality and AI:** Enhancing the World Around Us

Augmented Reality (AR) combined with AI can change how we interact with the world around us. From education and training to entertainment and shopping, AR can overlay information onto the real world in ways that are interactive and contextually relevant, powered by AI's understanding of objects and environments.

PRACTICAL AI PROJECTS

Diving into Artificial Intelligence (AI) projects is like assembling a toolbox that helps you build incredible things. Just as a carpenter needs hammers, saws, and nails, an AI enthusiast or developer requires various tools and libraries to bring their projects to life. These resources range from software that can analyze vast amounts of data to frameworks that help you train models to perform tasks like recognizing images or understanding human language. Let's explore some of the practical AI project tools and libraries that are essential for anyone looking to step into the world of AI.

Python: The AI Craftsman's Language

Think of Python as the universal language of AI development. It's like the duct tape in your toolbox – versatile and can fix or build almost anything. Python is favoured for its simplicity, readability, and the vast array of libraries and frameworks it supports for AI and machine learning (ML).

Libraries and Frameworks for Machine Learning

TensorFlow and Keras

TensorFlow is like the electric drill of your toolbox, powerful and precise for drilling into complex data and building sophisticated ML models. Developed by Google, it's used for both research and production needs.

Keras operates on top of TensorFlow like a drill bit that fits into your electric drill, making it easier to use and more accessible for beginners. It's perfect for prototyping and experimenting with neural networks.

PyTorch

Developed by Facebook, PyTorch is akin to a versatile saw that can cut through data in various ways, making it especially popular in academia and research for its flexibility and dynamic computational graph.

Scikit-learn

For more traditional, structured data tasks (like deciding whether to bring an umbrella based on the weather forecast), Scikit-learn is your go-to hammer. It's straightforward, effective, and can handle a wide range of ML tasks from clustering to regression and classification.

Data Analysis and Visualization

Pandas

Pandas are like a measuring tape, helping you to organize and make sense of your data. It's essential for data manipulation and analysis, allowing you to clean, filter, and prepare your data for modelling.

Matplotlib and Seaborn

Matplotlib and Seaborn are like your paintbrushes, allowing you to visualize data and the results of your AI models clearly and beautifully. They help in understanding data trends and patterns through graphical representation.

Natural Language Processing (NLP)

NLTK and spaCy

When dealing with human language data, NLTK (Natural Language Toolkit) and spaCy are invaluable tools. Think of them as the chisel and file in your toolbox, shaping and refining raw text data into a structured form that AI models can understand and process.

Deep Learning for Computer Vision

OpenCV

For projects involving image recognition or processing, OpenCV acts as your magnifying glass, helping you to see and understand images at a deeper level. It's widely used for tasks like object detection, face recognition, and video processing.

Reinforcement Learning

Gym

The gym, developed by OpenAI, is like a training ground or a simulator for your AI models. It provides various environments where you can train your AI agents to learn tasks such as playing video games or robotic control through trial and error.

Collaboration and Version Control

GitHub

Finally, GitHub is like the notebook of your toolbox, where you keep all your project blueprints safe and shareable. It's crucial for version control, collaboration, and showcasing your AI projects to the world.

Conclusion

Embarking on AI projects is an exciting journey, made significantly easier with the right set of tools and libraries. From Python, which serves as the foundation, to specialized libraries for tasks like machine learning, data visualization, and natural language processing, each tool in your AI toolbox serves a specific purpose. By leveraging these resources, you can turn raw data into insights, automate tasks, and even create systems that mimic human intelligence. Whether you're a beginner or looking to deepen your expertise in AI, familiarizing yourself with these tools and libraries is a step towards building innovative and impactful AI projects.

IMAGE CLASSIFICATION WITH CNN

Embarking on an image classification project using Convolutional Neural Networks (CNNs) is akin to teaching a computer to distinguish between different types of objects in photos, much like how you might teach a child to differentiate between cats and dogs by showing them pictures. This project will guide you through creating a simple CNN model to classify images. We'll use Python and TensorFlow, a popular machine-learning library, to build our model.

Setting Up Your Toolbox

Before we start, ensure you have Python installed on your computer. You'll also need TensorFlow, which can be installed using pip, Python's package manager. Open your command line or terminal and run:

```
pip install tensorflow
```

This command installs TensorFlow, including Keras, which is a high-level neural network API that TensorFlow includes for easy model building.

Preparing the Data: Cats vs. Dogs

For this project, let's teach our computer to distinguish between images of cats and dogs. TensorFlow includes a dataset called **cats_vs_dogs** that we can use for this purpose.

First, import the necessary libraries and the dataset:

```python
import tensorflow as tf
from tensorflow.keras import layers, models
from tensorflow.keras.preprocessing.image import ImageDataGenerator
import os

# Load the cats_vs_dogs dataset
(train_images, train_labels), (test_images, test_labels) = tf.keras.datasets.cats_vs_
```

```python
# Load the cats_vs_dogs dataset
(train_images, train_labels), (test_images, test_labels) = tf.keras.datasets.cats_vs_dogs.load_data()
```

Preprocessing the Data

Before feeding the images into the CNN, they need to be resized to a uniform size and scaled so their pixel values are between 0 and 1. This makes it easier for CNN to process them.

```python
# Define image dimensions and batch size
img_height, img_width = 150, 150
batch_size = 32

# Create an ImageDataGenerator for data augmentation
train_datagen = ImageDataGenerator(rescale=1./255,
                                   rotation_range=40,
                                   width_shift_range=0.2,
                                   height_shift_range=0.2,
                                   shear_range=0.2,
                                   zoom_range=0.2,
                                   horizontal_flip=True,
                                   fill_mode='nearest')

test_datagen = ImageDataGenerator(rescale=1./255)  # Note that we should not augment

# Flow training images in batches using train_datagen
train_generator = train_datagen.flow(train_images, train_labels, batch_size=batch_siz
test_generator = test_datagen.flow(test_images, test_labels, batch_size=batch_size)
```

```python
# Flow training images in batches using train_datagen
train_generator = train_datagen.flow(train_images, train_labels, batch_size=batch_size)
test_generator = test_datagen.flow(test_images, test_labels, batch_size=batch_size)
```

Building the CNN Model

Now, let's construct our CNN model. Think of a CNN as a pipeline where an image goes through various filters and operations to determine its class (cat or dog in this case).

```python
model = models.Sequential([
    # The first convolution and max pooling layer
    layers.Conv2D(32, (3,3), activation='relu', input_shape=(150, 150, 3)),
    layers.MaxPooling2D(2,2),
    # The second convolution and max pooling layer
    layers.Conv2D(64, (3,3), activation='relu'),
    layers.MaxPooling2D(2,2),
    # The third convolution and max pooling layer
    layers.Conv2D(128, (3,3), activation='relu'),
    layers.MaxPooling2D(2,2),
    # Flatten the results to feed into a DNN
    layers.Flatten(),
    # 512 neuron hidden layer
    layers.Dense(512, activation='relu'),
    # Output layer with a single neuron since it's a binary classification
    layers.Dense(1, activation='sigmoid')
])

model.compile(optimizer='adam',
              loss='binary_crossentropy',
              metrics=['accuracy'])
```

Training the Model

With the model built, it's time to train it with our images. This process involves showing the images to the model, letting it make predictions, and then adjusting the model's parameters based on the accuracy of those predictions.

```python
history = model.fit(train_generator,
                    steps_per_epoch=100,  # The number of batch iterations before a
                    epochs=15,
                    validation_data=test_generator,
                    validation_steps=50)  # The number of batch iterations before a
```

history = model.fit(train_generator, steps_per_epoch=100, # The number of batch iterations before a training epoch is considered finished. epochs=15,

validation_data=test_generator, validation_steps=50) # The number of batch iterations before a validation epoch is considered finished.

Evaluating the Model

After training the model, you can evaluate its performance on the test set to see how well it learned to classify images of cats and dogs.

```
test_loss, test_acc = model.evaluate(test_generator, steps=50)
print('Test accuracy:', test_acc)
```

What's Happening Here?

- **Convolutional and pooling layers:** These layers help the model detect patterns like edges, textures, and more complex features in the images. Each convolutional layer looks for specific features, and the pooling layers reduce the dimensionality of the data, making the model more efficient.

- **Flatten and Dense layers:** After extracting features with the convolutional layers, we flatten the output and feed it into a densely connected neural network for classification.

- **Training the model:** During training, the model learns to associate certain features (like shapes and patterns) with each class (cat or dog).

- **Evaluating the model:** We measure the model's accuracy on data it hasn't seen before to ensure it's learned to generalize and not just memorize the training data.

Through this project, you've seen how to use CNNs to classify images. This is just the tip of the iceberg, and as you dive deeper into AI, you'll discover more complex models and techniques for a wide range of tasks.

TEXT GENERATION WITH RECURRENT NEURAL NETWORKS (RNNS)

Exploring text generation with Recurrent Neural Networks (RNNs), specifically using Long Short-Term Memory (LSTM) networks, is akin to teaching a machine to write poetry or compose stories. These types of networks are adept at learning patterns in sequences of data, which makes them ideal for text generation. Let's dive into a simple project that illustrates how you can use Python and TensorFlow to teach a computer to generate text, character by character.

Setting Up Your Environment

Before you start, you need to set up your environment with the necessary tools. Python is our programming language of choice, and TensorFlow will be the framework providing the LSTM capabilities.

To install TensorFlow, run this command in your terminal or command prompt:

```
pip install tensorflow
```

Preparing the Data

For this project, let's use a dataset of Shakespeare's writing to train our LSTM. This choice is due to the rich structure and complexity of the text, which provides a good challenge for our LSTM model. You can find text datasets like Shakespeare's writings online, or you might choose any large text file that interests you.

First, load the text and prepare it for training:

```python
import tensorflow as tf

# Load the entire text
path_to_file = tf.keras.utils.get_file('shakespeare.txt', 'https://path_to_shakespear
text = open(path_to_file, 'rb').read().decode(encoding='utf-8')

# The unique characters in the file
vocab = sorted(set(text))
print(f'{len(vocab)} unique characters')
```

Load the entire text path_to_file = tf.keras.utils.get_file('shakespeare.txt', 'https://path_to_shakespeare.txt')

Encoding the Text

Since neural networks do not understand raw text, we need to convert characters to numbers. We'll create two lookup tables: one for converting characters to integers, and one for integers back to characters.

```python
char2idx = {char:idx for idx, char in enumerate(vocab)}
idx2char = np.array(vocab)

# Now we use the lookup table to convert the entire text to its numeric representation
text_as_int = np.array([char2idx[char] for char in text])
```

Now we use the lookup table to convert the entire text to its numeric representation text_as_int = np. array([char2idx[char] for char in text])

Creating Training Examples

LSTM networks expect input sequences and corresponding targets. Here, we'll create a sequence for training:

```python
seq_length = 100  # length of sequence for a training example
examples_per_epoch = len(text)//(seq_length+1)

# Create training examples / targets
char_dataset = tf.data.Dataset.from_tensor_slices(text_as_int)

sequences = char_dataset.batch(seq_length+1, drop_remainder=True)

def split_input_target(chunk):
    input_text = chunk[:-1]
    target_text = chunk[1:]
    return input_text, target_text

dataset = sequences.map(split_input_target)
```

Building the Model

Now, let's build a simple LSTM model for this task using tf. keras:

```python
# Length of the vocabulary in chars
vocab_size = len(vocab)

# The embedding dimension
embedding_dim = 256

# Number of RNN units
rnn_units = 1024

def build_model(vocab_size, embedding_dim, rnn_units, batch_size):
    model = tf.keras.Sequential([
        tf.keras.layers.Embedding(vocab_size, embedding_dim, batch_input_shape=[batch
        tf.keras.layers.LSTM(rnn_units, return_sequences=True, stateful=True, recurre
        tf.keras.layers.Dense(vocab_size)
    ])
    return model

model = build_model(vocab_size=len(vocab), embedding_dim=embedding_dim, rnn_units=rn
```

def build_model(vocab_size, embedding_dim, rnn_units, batch_size): model = tf.keras.Sequential([

tf.keras.layers.Embedding(vocab_size, embedding_dim, batch_input_shape=[batch_size, None]),

tf.keras.layers.LSTM(rnn_units, return_sequences=True, stateful=True, recurrent_initializer='glorot_uniform'),

tf.keras.layers.Dense(vocab_size)])

return model

model = build_model(vocab_size=len(vocab), embedding_dim=embedding_dim, rnn_units=rnn_units, batch_size=64)

Train the Model

You will compile and train the model, which might take some time depending on your hardware:

```python
model.compile(optimizer='adam', loss=tf.keras.losses.SparseCategoricalCrossentropy(f
history = model.fit(dataset, epochs=30)
```

```python
model.compile(optimizer='adam',
loss=tf.keras.losses.SparseCategoricalCrossentropy(from_logits=True))

history = model.fit(dataset, epochs=30)
```

Generate Text

Finally, you can use the trained model to generate text:

```python
def generate_text(model, start_string):
    num_generate = 1000  # number of characters to generate

    input_eval = [char2idx[s] for s in start_string]
    input_eval = tf.expand_dims(input_eval, 0)

    text_generated = []

    model.reset_states()
    for i in range(num_generate):
        predictions = model(input_eval)
        predictions = tf.squeeze(predictions, 0)

        predicted_id = tf.random.categorical(predictions, num_samples=1)[-1,0].numpy()
        input_eval = tf.expand_dims([predicted_id], 0)

        text_generated.append(idx2char[predicted_id])

    return (start_string + ''.join(text_generated))

# Pass any starting string to generate text
print(generate_text(model, start_string=u"ROMEO: "))
```

```
for i in range(num_generate):

    predictions = model(input_eval)

    predictions = tf.squeeze(predictions, 0)

    predicted_id = tf.random.categorical(predictions, num_samples=1)[-1,0].numpy()

    input_eval = tf.expand_dims([predicted_id], 0)

    text_generated.append(idx2char[predicted_id])
return (start_string + ''.join(text_generated))
```

What's Happening Here?

Training: The model learns the patterns of language in Shakespeare's text, predicting the next character based on a sequence of characters.

Generation: We seed the model with a starting string, and then it generates text character by character based on what it learned during training.

This LSTM model provides a basic framework for generating text using character-based prediction, which you can extend and improve in various ways, such as by training on different datasets, tweaking the model architecture, or experimenting with the training process to achieve better results.

GENERATIVE AI

Generative AI is a branch of artificial intelligence that focuses on creating new content, such as images, music, text, or even videos. It uses advanced algorithms to learn from a large amount of data, and then it uses this learning to generate new, original pieces that resemble the data it studied but are completely new creations.

Here's a simple breakdown of how generative deep learning works and why it's exciting:

What Does "Generative" Mean?

"Generative" refers to the capability of these algorithms to produce or create something. Unlike other AI models that might predict the next word in a sentence or classify images(like telling a cat from a dog), generative models are all about making new examples that look like they could fit right into the original dataset.

How Does Generative Deep Learning Work?

1. **Learning from Examples:** First, the model looks at a lot of examples. For instance, if the task is to generate new images of dogs, the model would first study thousands of dog pictures to understand how dogs look.

2. **Understanding Patterns:** As it learns, the model picks up on patterns and important features—like shapes, sizes, colours, and positions—that define what makes a dog look like a dog.

3. **Creating New Images:** Once it has learned enough, the model can then start generating new images of dogs that don't exist but look realistic enough to be mistaken for real photos.

Types of Generative Models

Two popular types of generative models are:

Generative Adversarial Networks (GANs): This type of model consists of two smaller models that compete against each other. One model generates new data, while the other judges if it's realistic. This competition improves both models, making the generated data increasingly realistic over time.

Variational Autoencoders (VAEs): These models learn to compress data into a smaller form and then uncompress it back to the original form. By modifying the compressed form slightly, they can generate new data that resembles the original data.

Why is Generative Deep Learning Important?

1. **Creativity:** It can create things that don't exist, opening up possibilities in art, design, and entertainment.

2. **Simulation:** It can simulate data for training other AI models when real data is scarce or expensive to collect.

3. **Problem-Solving:** It helps in solving complex problems by generating a variety of solutions and testing which one might work best.

Conclusion

Think of generative deep learning as a school where the model is a student. This student watches a teacher (the dataset) do something many times—like drawing pictures of cats. After many lessons, the student (the AI model) tries to draw their cat pictures without copying any existing ones, using what it has learned about what cats look like. The goal is for these new drawings to be good enough that they look like they could have been drawn by the teacher.

Generative deep learning is exciting because it's like teaching a computer to be creative, and to make new things after learning about old things, which opens up many possibilities for both practical applications and artistic endeavours.

UNDERSTANDING ADVANCED GENERATIVE ADVERSARIAL NETWORKS (GANS)

Generative Adversarial Networks (GANs) are a cutting-edge technology in the field of artificial intelligence that focus on generating new content, such as images, videos, and even sound, that mimics the real world. Initially introduced by Ian Goodfellow and his colleagues in 2014, GANs have since undergone significant improvements and diversifications, leading to more stable and high-quality results. Let's delve into how these networks work, their advanced variants like Wasserstein GANs and StyleGANs, and explore their applications, particularly in creating realistic images and videos.

Basic Concept of GANs

At its core, a GAN consists of two main components:

1. **Generator:** This component generates new data instances.
2. **Discriminator:** This component evaluates the authenticity of the generated data, determining whether each instance of data it reviews is real (drawn from the actual dataset) or fake (created by the generator).

The generator and discriminator are trained simultaneously in a game-theoretic approach where the generator aims to increasingly fool the discriminator, and the discriminator strives to become better at distinguishing real from fake.

Advanced Variants of GANs

As GANs developed, several issues became apparent, such as training instability and the generation of unrealistic samples. Advanced models like Wasserstein GANs (WGANs) and StyleGANs have been introduced to address these issues.

Wasserstein GANs (WGANs)

Wasserstein GANs introduce a new approach to measure the difference between the distribution of the data generated by the generator and the real data distribution. This method, based on the Wasserstein distance, provides a more meaningful and smooth gradient to the generator, unlike traditional GANs that use the Jensen-Shannon divergence. This change helps in:

1. Reducing training instability by providing more useful gradients throughout the training process.

2. Preventing mode collapse where the generator generates a limited diversity of samples.

StyleGANs

Developed by researchers at NVIDIA, StyleGANs introduce an alternative architecture that can manipulate high-level attributes and stochastic variation in the generated images (like hairstyles in portraits or certain textures in landscapes). StyleGANs use a mapping network to translate input noise variables into an intermediate latent space that controls specific features of the generated image, allowing precise control over the synthesis process. The latest version, StyleGAN3, introduced improvements that make the generated images more realistic by enhancing rotational and translational equivariance.

Applications of Advanced GANs

1. Artistic Creation and Design

Advanced GANs are extensively used in creative fields to produce artwork and design elements that are both innovative and aesthetically pleasing. Artists and designers can experiment with different styles and forms without the need to manually sketch every new idea.

2. Entertainment Industry

In the entertainment sector, GANs revolutionize the way visual content is created. For instance, in filmmaking, GANs can generate realistic backgrounds and special effects, reducing the reliance on expensive and time-consuming physical sets or CGI techniques.

3. Advertising

The advertising industry benefits from GANs through the creation of dynamic visual content that is tailored to specific audiences. This technology can generate variations of the same ad to appeal to different demographics and personal preferences.

4. Video Games and Virtual Reality

GANs contribute to the development of more realistic environments in video games and virtual reality, enhancing user immersion. They can generate detailed textures and landscapes, improving the visual quality and responsiveness of virtual worlds.

5. **Training and Simulation**

In sectors where training data may be limited or sensitive (like medical imaging), GANs can generate additional data for training purposes. This helps in creating robust models without the need for extensive real-world data collection.

Recent Innovations and Updates as of 2024

As of 2024, GAN technology continues to evolve with enhancements that focus on improving realism, reducing computational costs, and ensuring ethical usage. Innovations include:

1. **Integration with other AI technologies:** Combining GANs with other AI forms like reinforcement learning to create systems that can learn from their environments and improve the generation process autonomously.
2. **Energy-efficient GANs:** Newer models are being developed to reduce the substantial energy requirements of training large GANs, making them more sustainable and accessible.
3. **Ethical and controlled generation:** With the increasing realism of GAN-generated images and videos, there is also a focus on developing mechanisms to ensure these technologies are used ethically, including watermarking synthetic content to distinguish it from real footage.

Conclusion

Advanced Generative Adversarial Networks continue to push the boundaries of what's possible in artificial intelligence, opening up new avenues for creativity, problem-solving, and innovation across various industries.

VARIATIONAL AUTOENCODERS (VAES)

Variational Autoencoders (VAEs) are a type of artificial intelligence used in the field of deep learning for generating complex data distributions. Since their introduction in 2013 by Kingma and Welling, VAEs have become a popular tool for creating realistic and diverse datasets, such as images of human faces, voices, or even styles of art. Let's delve into how VAEs work, explore their advancements, and discuss their applications, especially in generating realistic human faces.

Basic Concept of VAEs

At its core, a VAE is a probabilistic spin on the traditional autoencoder—a type of neural network that learns to compress (encode) data into a lower-dimensional space and then decompress (decode) it back to the original form. The VAE introduces a probabilistic twist by not learning to encode an input into a fixed point, but rather into a distribution over possible points from which the input could have been generated.

Key Components of a VAE

- **Encoder:** This part of the VAE learns to take the input data and translate it into two parameters in a latent space—means and variances. These parameters define a probability distribution believed to have generated the input data.
- **Decoder:** The decoder then samples points from this distribution and attempts to reconstruct the input data from these samples.

How VAEs Differ from Traditional Autoencoders:

- **Probabilistic Nature:** Unlike traditional autoencoders that map input data to a single fixed point, VAEs map inputs to a distribution, allowing for the generation of new data points.
- **Regularisation:** VAEs inherently manage the encoding space (latent space) to ensure that similar data points are mapped close together, which helps in generating coherent and realistic samples.

Advancements in VAE Technology

Over the past decade, VAEs have seen several advancements that enhance their stability, efficiency, and applicability:

Improved Sampling Techniques

Advances in sampling methods have allowed VAEs to generate higher quality and more varied data. Techniques like importance-weighted autoencoders (IWAE) improve the training by taking multiple samples from the latent space, which helps the model learn more robust distributions.

Conditional VAEs

Conditional VAEs (CVAEs) are an extension where the generation process is conditioned on additional information, such as labels. This allows the model to generate targeted outputs, such as a face with specific attributes (e.g., smiling, eyes open).

Hybrid Models

Combining VAEs with other types of networks, such as GANs, has led to models that can leverage the strengths of both. For example, the VAE/GAN hybrid uses the VAE's powerful generative capabilities with the GAN's sharpness and detail in generation, enhancing the realism of generated images.

Applications of VAEs

Generating Realistic Human Faces

One of the most striking applications of VAEs is in the generation of human faces. These models can create new faces that do not correspond to real individuals but look nearly indistinguishable from real human photos. This has applications in areas such as:

1. **Entertainment and Gaming:** Creating characters for video games and animations without the need for manual design.
2. **Training Data:** Generating diverse human faces for training facial recognition systems.

Fashion and Design

VAEs are used in the fashion industry to design new clothing items by learning the distribution of existing designs and generating new variations that keep to current trends yet introduce novel design elements.

Healthcare

In healthcare, VAEs generate realistic, anonymized datasets of human faces or other body parts for research and training purposes without using real patient data, addressing privacy concerns.

Recent Updates and Innovations as of 2024

As of 2024, VAE technology has continued to evolve with a focus on improving the detail and accuracy of generated data, as well as the efficiency of the models:

Enhanced Resolution and Detail

Recent models can generate images with significantly higher resolution and detail due to improvements in network architecture and training techniques, making the outputs more realistic.

Speed and Efficiency

Enhancements in hardware and training algorithms have reduced the computational requirements for training VAEs, making high-quality models accessible to more users and applications.

Ethical and Responsible Use

With the increasing capability of VAEs to generate realistic human data, there has been a concurrent rise in ethical considerations and guidelines to prevent the misuse of synthetic media, particularly in ensuring that generated data is used responsibly in public domains.

Conclusion

Variational Autoencoders have revolutionized the way we think about generating realistic and complex data distributions. From creating lifelike human faces to aiding in medical research, VAEs have broadened the scope of what can be achieved with artificial intelligence, providing tools that both inspire innovation and challenge our ethical frameworks. As we move forward, the balance of these advancements with responsible usage will be crucial in shaping the future of generative models.

UNDERSTANDING TRANSFORMER ARCHITECTURES

Transformer architectures have revolutionized the field of artificial intelligence, particularly in tasks involving natural language processing (NLP) and, more recently, in computer vision and other areas. Introduced in the paper "Attention is All You Need" by Vaswani et al. in 2017, Transformers introduced a novel approach to handling sequential data that moved away from the traditional recurrent neural network (RNN) models. This new architecture is built around the concept of self-attention, which allows it to process input data in parallel and capture complex relationships within the data.

Core Components of Transformer Architectures

Self-Attention Mechanism

The heart of a Transformer is the self-attention mechanism. Unlike previous models that processed data sequentially (one element at a time), the self-attention mechanism allows the model to look at different positions of the input sequence simultaneously. This capability helps the model understand the context around each word (or pixel in the case of images) in a sentence (or image), regardless of their distance from each other in the sequence.

How Self-Attention Works: The mechanism computes three vectors from each input: the Query, Key, and Value. For each input element, self-attention computes a score that indicates how much focus to place on other parts of the input sequence. This score is calculated by taking the dot product of the Query vector with the Key vector of the other inputs. The scores determine how much each part of the input should attend to the other parts, allowing the model to dynamically prioritize which parts of the input are most relevant to each other.

Multi-Head Attention

To refine the self-attention process further, Transformers use what is called multi-head attention. This involves running several self-attention processes in parallel, each with its own independent sets of Queries, Keys, and Values. The outputs of these parallel processes are then concatenated and linearly transformed into the desired dimension. This multi-head approach allows the model to capture different types of relationships from different representational spaces at different positions in the sequence, providing a more comprehensive understanding of the input.

Positional Encoding

Since the self-attention mechanism does not inherently consider the position of the elements in the sequence, Transformers add positional encodings to the input embeddings to incorporate information about the position of each element in the sequence. Positional encodings can be either learned or fixed and are added to the input embeddings before processing by the attention layers. This addition ensures that the model maintains an awareness of the order of the sequence, which is crucial for tasks like language translation.

Transformer Model Architecture

A standard Transformer model comprises two main parts: the encoder and the decoder, each made up of multiple identical layers.

Encoder

The encoder processes the input data in parallel through its layers. Each layer has two sub-layers: a multi-head self-attention mechanism and a position-wise fully connected feed-forward network. A residual connection is employed around each of these sub-layers, followed by layer normalization. This structure helps in maintaining the flow of gradients during training, which is critical for training deep networks.

Decoder

The decoder is also composed of layers that, in addition to the two sub-layers present in the encoder layers, have a third sub-layer that performs multi-head attention over the encoder's output. This structure allows the decoder to focus on appropriate portions of the input sequence, aiding tasks like summarization or translation where the output depends on selective parts of the input.

Applications and Impact

Transformer architectures are not only more efficient but also generally more effective than their predecessors at tasks involving large amounts of data and long-range dependencies. They have set new benchmarks in a variety of NLP tasks such as translation, text summarization, and sentiment analysis. Beyond NLP, Transformers are being adapted for use in other domains like image recognition and even music generation, showcasing their versatility and powerful capability to model complex patterns.

UNDERSTANDING TRANSFORMER MODELS IN GENERATIVE TASKS

Transformer models, since their introduction in 2017 by Vaswani et al., have revolutionized the field of natural language processing (NLP). They are designed to handle sequential data like text but in a way that is different from previous models. Unlike traditional models that process data in sequence, one word after another, Transformers process all words at once. This allows them to understand the context better and faster. Models like BERT (Bidirectional Encoder Representations from Transformers) and GPT (Generative Pre-trained Transformer) are at the forefront of this revolution, significantly enhancing how machines understand and generate human language.

Core Principles of Transformer Models

Parallel Processing

Transformers use a mechanism called self-attention, which allows them to weigh the importance of each word in a sentence, regardless of its position. This means they can process all words in a sentence simultaneously, rather than one by one. This not only speeds up the training but also improves the model's ability to handle long-range dependencies in text.

Scalability

Due to their parallel nature, Transformer models scale particularly well with increased data and computational power. This scalability is a key reason why newer versions of these models (like GPT-3 and beyond) have dramatically increased in size and capability, managing billions of parameters effectively.

Innovations in Transformer Models

BERT (Bidirectional Encoder Representations from Transformers)

Developed by Google, BERT has changed the way we approach tasks such as language understanding, sentiment analysis, and question answering. Unlike previous models that read text in one direction (either left-to-right or right-to-left), BERT reads text in both directions simultaneously. This bi-directionality allows the model to understand the context better, which is crucial for understanding the meaning of words in different situations.

Impact on NLP Tasks:

1. **Language Understanding:** BERT has set new standards for language understanding benchmarks. It helps machines understand nuances in language, including slang and colloquial expressions, much more effectively.
2. **Text Classification:** From categorizing entire documents to classifying individual words based on their meanings, BERT has improved accuracy across various text classification tasks.
3. **Search Engines:** Google uses BERT to enhance search results by understanding the context of search queries better, leading to more relevant results for users.

GPT (Generative Pre-trained Transformer)

While BERT excels at understanding language, GPT focuses on generating text. Developed by OpenAI, GPT is a series of models trained on a diverse internet dataset to generate text from prompts. GPT-3, one of the latest in the series, can compose poetry, draft emails, summarize long documents, and even code simple software applications.

Impact on NLP Tasks:

1. **Content Creation:** GPT models are used by businesses to generate high-quality written content quickly, aiding content marketers and social media managers.
2. **Translation:** Despite not being trained specifically to translate languages, GPT models can perform translations by understanding context and generating appropriate text in another language.
3. **Educational Tools:** GPT can power tutoring systems that provide explanations to students, help with homework, and even simulate conversation practice in different languages.

Advanced Training Techniques

As of 2024, techniques such as diffusion models have been integrated into the training processes of Transformers, improving their efficiency and effectiveness. These techniques help in refining the models further, allowing them to generate more nuanced text and better handle ambiguities in language.

Energy Efficiency

There has been a significant push towards making Transformer models more energy-efficient. Innovations in hardware and model design have reduced the energy costs associated with training and running these models, making them more sustainable and accessible.

Ethical and Responsible AI

With great power comes great responsibility. The latest developments in Transformer models also include better frameworks for dealing with biases in the models and ensuring they are used ethically. Efforts are being made to make these models transparent and accountable, especially when used in sensitive areas like healthcare and law enforcement.

Conclusion

Transformer models have drastically transformed the landscape of NLP, providing tools that understand and generate human language with unprecedented accuracy and fluency. As these models continue to evolve, they hold the promise of further blurring the lines between human and machine capabilities in processing and generating language. The focus remains on harnessing their power responsibly, ensuring that as these models learn more about us, they do so in a way that is beneficial and ethical.

TRANSFER LEARNING AND FINE-TUNING

In the world of Natural Language Processing (NLP), the advent of transfer learning and fine-tuning has marked a significant shift in how models are developed and deployed. These techniques allow for remarkable flexibility and efficiency, transforming the landscape of AI by enabling a model trained on one task to excel at others with minimal additional training. This evolution has been pivotal, especially as the demand for sophisticated NLP applications continues to grow in various sectors.

Understanding Transfer Learning and Fine-Tuning

Transfer Learning: The Concept

Transfer learning is a method where knowledge gained while solving one problem is applied to a different but related problem. For instance, a model trained to recognize speech in English might be adapted to recognize French. In NLP, this approach involves taking a model that has been pre-trained on a large dataset and reusing it on a new, often smaller and more specific dataset. The underlying idea is that the pre-trained model has already learned a significant amount of relevant information about language in general, which can be effectively transferred to new tasks.

Fine-Tuning: The Strategy

Fine-tuning is a specific type of transfer learning. After a model has been pre-trained on a large dataset, fine-tuning involves making slight adjustments to the model's parameters to tailor it to a particular task. This is typically done by continuing the training process on a new dataset with a smaller learning rate, allowing the model to adjust to the specifics of the new data while retaining the knowledge it gained during pre-training. This process is much faster and requires significantly less data than training a model from scratch.

Revolutionizing NLP with Transfer Learning and Fine-Tuning

The introduction of models like BERT (Bidirectional Encoder Representations from Transformers) and GPT (Generative Pre-trained Transformer) has underscored the effectiveness of transfer learning and fine-tuning in NLP. These models, trained on vast amounts of text data, have shown unparalleled ability in understanding and generating language.

Reduced Need for Large Datasets

One of the most significant impacts of transfer learning and fine-tuning in NLP is the reduced necessity for large, task-specific datasets. Traditionally, training an NLP model from scratch requires substantial amounts of labelled data, which is expensive and time-consuming to gather. Transfer learning allows researchers and developers to leverage existing pre-trained models, drastically reducing the need for new data and speeding up the development process.

Improved Model Performance

Models that are fine-tuned from pre-trained systems often outperform those trained from scratch, even when they use much smaller datasets. This is because the pre-trained model brings with it a foundational understanding of language, including syntax, grammar, and even some level of semantic knowledge, which provides a significant headstart in learning new tasks.

Versatility Across Different Tasks

Transfer learning and fine-tuning have proven effective across a broad spectrum of NLP tasks, from text classification and sentiment analysis to question-answering and language translation. This versatility makes it an invaluable approach in an industry where new applications and needs are constantly emerging.

Case Studies and Applications

1. **Sentiment Analysis:** Companies use fine-tuned models to gauge public sentiment on social media about products or services.

2. **Legal Document Analysis:** Law firms employ these techniques to automate the extraction of relevant information from legal documents.

3. **Language Translation Services:** Translation apps use models initially trained on one language pair and fine-tune them for others to provide quick and accurate translations.

Challenges and Considerations

While transfer learning and fine-tuning offer substantial benefits, they also come with challenges. The process requires careful management to avoid issues like catastrophic forgetting, where a model forgets what it learned in its initial training. Moreover, the success of fine-tuning can heavily depend on how similar the new task is to the tasks the model was originally trained on.

Conclusion

Transfer learning and fine-tuning are fundamentally changing the landscape of NLP by providing a way to leverage previously acquired knowledge for new tasks. This not only enhances model performance but also reduces the resources and time required for model training. As these techniques continue to develop, they promise to unlock even greater capabilities and applications in NLP, making advanced language understanding and generation more accessible across industries.

ADVANCEMENTS IN MACHINE TRANSLATION: A FOCUS ON NEURAL NETWORKS AND LOW-RESOURCE LANGUAGES

Machine translation, the process of using computers to translate text or speech from one language to another, has seen dramatic improvements in recent years, particularly with the advent of neural networks. These advancements are especially significant for low-resource languages—languages that typically have less digital data available and have historically been underrepresented in translation technologies. This shift not only enhances communication across global boundaries but also preserves linguistic diversity in the digital age.

Understanding Neural Networks in Translation

Neural networks are a type of artificial intelligence that mimics the way human brains operate, allowing machines to learn from large amounts of data. In the context of machine translation, neural networks, specifically those designed as deep learning models, have become the backbone of the most advanced systems. These models use layers of algorithms to analyze and learn from vast amounts of language data, gradually improving their translation accuracy through exposure and adjustments.

Key Components of Neural Machine Translation:

1. **Encoder-Decoder Architecture:** This setup is fundamental in neural machine translation. The encoder processes the input text, converting it into a digital format that the model can understand, often referred to as the "context vector." The decoder then takes this vector and generates the translated text in the target language.

2. **Attention Mechanisms:** These allow the translation model to focus on different parts of the input sentence as it generates each word of the output. This feature is crucial for maintaining the context and improving the fluidity and accuracy of the translation.

Recent Breakthroughs in Translation Quality

Enhanced Contextual Understanding

Recent models have improved in understanding the context, not just the text. Advanced neural networks, especially those utilizing transformer models like BERT (Bidirectional Encoder Representations from Transformers) and GPT (Generative Pre-trained

Transformer), handle nuances and idiomatic expressions much better than earlier systems. This ability to grasp context has significantly boosted accuracy in translation.

Real-Time Translation

Developments in hardware and software optimization have enabled real-time translation, which is transformative for live interactions, international conferences, and customer support across languages. This technology uses powerful neural networks that can process and translate speech as it happens, breaking down language barriers in real time.

Focusing on Low-Resource Languages

One of the most impactful advancements in machine translation has been the increased attention to low-resource languages. These languages, which may have limited textual resources available for training traditional models, are now being supported better due to several innovations:

1. **Transfer Learning:** Techniques that transfer knowledge from high-resource languages to low-resource ones have proven effective. By using models pre-trained on languages with extensive data, researchers can fine-tune them on smaller datasets of low-resource languages, significantly improving translation quality without the need for vast corpora.

2. **Crowdsourced Data Generation:** Initiatives to increase the amount of training data for low-resource languages through crowdsourcing have also gained momentum. This approach involves users contributing translations to help train the models, effectively increasing the data pool.

3. **Multilingual Models:** Recent neural networks are designed to handle multiple languages simultaneously. These multilingual models can share knowledge across languages, which is particularly beneficial for related languages, allowing them to leverage common linguistic features.

Case Studies

1. **Google Translate:** Continues to add support for more languages, using advanced AI to provide better translations for languages that were previously very poorly supported.

2. **Facebook's M2M-100:** A machine translation model that can translate directly between any pair of 100 languages without relying on English as an intermediary, which improves the quality of low-resource languages by preserving nuances lost in double translation.

Challenges and Future Directions

Despite these advancements, challenges remain. Issues such as handling languages with different syntax or those that use a non-Latin script are ongoing areas of research. Moreover, ethical concerns about data privacy in the collection of linguistic data for training purposes continue to be a topic of debate.

Conclusion

The advancements in machine translation powered by neural networks have significantly changed the landscape, particularly for low-resource languages. These improvements not only enhance communication and accessibility but also contribute to the preservation of global cultural diversity. As technology continues to evolve, the future of machine translation looks promising, with ongoing research likely to solve existing challenges and open up even more possibilities for seamless cross-lingual interaction.

NLP FOR ENTERPRISE APPLICATIONS: INTEGRATING ADVANCED LANGUAGE UNDERSTANDING IN BUSINESS

Natural Language Processing (NLP) is rapidly becoming a cornerstone of enterprise technology, transforming how businesses interact with customers, manage data, and drive decision-making. As of 2024, NLP has seen substantial innovations and integrations in various business applications, including sentiment analysis, customer service automation, and beyond. This detailed exploration covers how NLP technologies are being employed in real-world scenarios, emphasizing case studies and the latest innovations.

Understanding Natural Language Processing in Enterprises

NLP involves teaching computers to understand, interpret, and generate human language in a way that is both valuable and meaningful. The technology uses algorithms to analyze, understand, and derive information from human language smartly and efficiently. For businesses, this capability opens up numerous avenues for enhancing operational efficiency and customer engagement.

Key Areas of NLP Application in Enterprises

Sentiment Analysis

Sentiment analysis uses NLP to analyze the emotions behind words. Businesses use this technology to gauge public opinion, monitor brand reputation, and understand customer experiences by analyzing data from social media, surveys, and other sources.

Real-World Application: A major retail company uses sentiment analysis to monitor customer reviews and social media mentions to gauge reactions to products and services. This helps them quickly address issues, adapt marketing strategies, and improve product offerings.

Customer Service Automation

NLP is revolutionizing customer service through chatbots and automated response systems that can understand and respond to customer queries in natural language.

Case Study: A leading telecommunications company implemented an NLP-powered chatbot to handle customer queries on its website. This bot handles millions of interactions each year, reducing wait times and freeing human agents to deal with more complex issues.

Automated Content Generation

NLP technologies enable the automated creation of content for reports, summaries, and even news articles, making the process faster and more cost-effective.

Innovation: A financial news outlet uses NLP to generate earnings reports and news articles based on financial data automatically. This allows them to publish content quickly after earnings are released, significantly faster than traditional methods.

Advancements in NLP Technologies for Enterprises

Language Models and Transformers

Recent advancements in NLP are largely driven by the development of sophisticated models like BERT and GPT-3. These models, based on the transformer architecture, have significantly improved the understanding and generation of human language by computers.

Impact: These models are used in customer service to understand the context of customer requests better and generate more accurate and relevant responses. For instance, GPT-3 can generate human-like responses, draft emails, and even code, reducing the time employees spend on routine tasks.

Multilingual Support

As global businesses need to operate across linguistic boundaries, NLP systems have expanded to offer multilingual support. This allows companies to deploy customer service and content generation applications in various languages without building separate solutions for each language.

Case Study: A multinational corporation uses a multilingual NLP system to provide customer support in over 20 languages, ensuring consistent quality of service across different regions without the need for a multilingual staff.

Real-Time Processing

Enhancements in hardware and optimization techniques have enabled real-time NLP processing, which is crucial for applications such as customer interactions and live sentiment analysis.

Application: During live product launches, a tech company uses real-time sentiment analysis to gather feedback from social media streams, helping marketing teams gauge public reaction instantly and adjust their strategies accordingly.

Challenges and Ethical Considerations

Despite these advancements, NLP implementation in enterprises is not without challenges. Issues such as data privacy, the need for large, annotated datasets for training models, and the management of bias in language understanding are critical considerations.

Ethical Concerns: As NLP technology can potentially access sensitive information, businesses must ensure they comply with data protection regulations and ethical guidelines, especially when handling customer data.

The Future of NLP in Business

Looking forward, NLP is set to deepen its integration into business operations. Areas like predictive analytics, where NLP can help predict trends from news articles and social media, and personalized marketing, where companies can tailor content based on customer sentiment and preferences, are expected to grow.

Conclusion

NLP is a transformative technology that is reshaping the landscape of business operations. Through applications in sentiment analysis, customer service, and automated content generation, businesses are not only improving efficiency but are also gaining deeper insights into their operations and their customers' needs. As NLP technology continues to evolve, its integration into enterprise applications is expected to become more profound, offering even greater benefits and new capabilities.

BUILDING A CUSTOMER SUPPORT AI BOT USING GOOGLE'S BERT

Creating an AI-powered customer support bot involves several key steps: setting up the environment, preprocessing data, training a model, and deploying the model. Here, we will use Google's BERT (Bidirectional Encoder Representations from Transformers) due to its effectiveness in understanding the context of user queries. This tutorial will guide you through each step, including the coding part, to build a functional AI customer support bot.

Step 1: Setting Up the Environment

Before we dive into coding, you'll need to set up your development environment. You should have Python installed on your system. Additionally, we'll use libraries like TensorFlow, Transformers, and Flask for the web application.

Installing Required Libraries

Open your command line interface (CLI) and run the following commands to install the necessary libraries:

```
pip install tensorflow
pip install transformers
pip install flask
```

Step 2: Preprocessing Data

The quality of your AI model greatly depends on the quality of the data it's trained on. For customer support, you'll need a dataset of customer queries and appropriate responses. For this example, let's assume you have a CSV file with two columns: query and response.

Sample Data Preparation

Here's a simple example of how your data might look:

query	response
What are your store hours?	Our store hours are 9am to 9pm.
How can I reset my password?	You can reset your password by clicking "Forgot password?" on the login page.

Loading and Preparing Data

Use pandas to load and prepare your data:

```python
import pandas as pd

# Load the dataset
data = pd.read_csv('customer_support_data.csv')

# Display the first few rows
print(data.head())
```

Step 3: Training the Model

To train the model, we'll use the Transformers library by Hugging Face, which provides a straightforward interface for working with BERT.

Loading BERT

First, load a pre-trained BERT model and the corresponding tokenizer:

```python
from transformers import BertTokenizer, TFBertForSequenceClassification
from transformers import InputExample, InputFeatures

model = TFBertForSequenceClassification.from_pretrained('bert-base-uncased')
tokenizer = BertTokenizer.from_pretrained('bert-base-uncased')
```

Converting Data into a Format BERT Can Understand

BERT requires data in a specific format. We will convert our customer support queries and responses into this format:

```python
def convert_data_to_examples(train, label):
    train_InputExamples = train.apply(lambda x: InputExample(guid=None,
                                                              text_a = x['query'],
                                                              text_b = None,
                                                              label = x['response']), a
    return train_InputExamples

def convert_examples_to_tf_dataset(examples, tokenizer, max_length=128):
    features = []
    for e in examples:
        input_dict = tokenizer.encode_plus(
            e.text_a,
            add_special_tokens=True,
            max_length=max_length,
            return_token_type_ids=True,
            return_attention_mask=True,
            pad_to_max_length=True,
            truncation=True
        )

        input_ids, token_type_ids, attention_mask = (input_dict["input_ids"],
            input_dict["token_type_ids"], input_dict['attention_mask'])

        features.append(
            InputFeatures(
                input_ids=input_ids, attention_mask=attention_mask, token_type_ids=t
            )
        )

    def gen():
        for f in features:
            yield (
                {
                    "input_ids": f.input_ids,
                    "attention_mask": f.attention_mask,
                    "token_type_ids": f.token_type_ids,
                },
                f.label,
            )

    return tf.data.Dataset.from_generator(
        gen,
        ({"input_ids": tf.int32, "attention_mask": tf.int32, "token_type_ids": tf.in
        (
            {"input_ids": tf.TensorShape([None]), "attention_mask": tf.TensorShape([
             tf.TensorShape([]),
        ),
    )

train_InputExamples = convert_data_to_examples(data, data.response)
train_data = convert_examples_to_tf_dataset(list(train_InputExamples), tokenizer)
train_data = train_data.shuffle(100).batch(32).repeat(2)
```

features.append(InputFeatures(input_ids=input_ids, attention_mask=attention_mask, token_type_ids=token_type_ids, label=e.label)) return tf.data.Dataset.from_generator(gen, ({"input_ids": tf.int32, "attention_mask": tf.int32, "token_type_ids": tf.int32}, tf.int64), ({"input_ids": tf.TensorShape([None]), "attention_mask": tf.TensorShape([None]), "token_type_ids": tf.TensorShape([None])}, tf.TensorShape([]),),)

Model Training

Now, train the model with the preprocessed data:

```python
model.compile(optimizer=tf.keras.optimizers.Adam(learning_rate=3e-5, epsilon=1e-08,
              loss=tf.keras.losses.SparseCategoricalCrossentropy(from_logits=True),
              metrics=[tf.keras.metrics.SparseCategoricalAccuracy('accuracy')])

model.fit(train_data, epochs=3, steps_per_epoch=115)
```

Step 4: Deploying the Model

After training, your model is ready to be deployed. We'll use Flask for a simple web application that interacts with the model.

Setting Up Flask Application

Create a new Python file, app.py, and set up a basic Flask application:

```python
from flask import Flask, request, jsonify
app = Flask(__name__)

@app.route('/predict', methods=['POST'])
def predict():
    query = request.json['query']
    inputs = tokenizer.encode(query, return_tensors="tf")
    outputs = model(inputs)[0]
    prediction = tf.argmax(outputs, axis=1).numpy()[0]
    response = data['response'][prediction]
    return jsonify(response=response)

if __name__ == '__main__':
    app.run(debug=True)
```

This Flask application provides an endpoint where you can send customer queries, and it will respond with the predicted response.

Conclusion

By following these steps, you have built an AI-powered customer support bot using Google's BERT. This bot can understand customer queries and respond appropriately, showcasing the practical application of advanced NLP techniques in real-world business scenarios. This example serves as a foundation, which can be further customized and improved to meet specific business needs, including handling more complex interactions and integrating with existing customer support systems.

www.ingramcontent.com/pod-product-compliance
Lightning Source LLC
Chambersburg PA
CBHW070259230526
45470CB00002B/647